52

PATHS

OF THE

PILGRIMS

AND LIVES OF THE

EARLY SAINTS

IN SCOTLAND

Mary McGrigor

D1337417

SCOTTISH CULTURAL PRESS

www.scottishbooks.com

First published in 2006 by
Scottish Cultural Press
Unit 6, Newbattle Abbey Business Park
Newbattle Road, Dalkeith EH22 3LJ Scotland
Tel: +44 (0)131 660 6366 • Fax: +44 (0)870 285 4846
Email: info@scottishbooks.com
website: **www.scottishbooks.com**

British Library Cataloguing in Publication Data
A catalogue record for this book is available
from the British Library

ISBN-10: 1 898218 82 X
ISBN-13: 978 1 898218 82 1

Printed and **bound** by
Athenæum Press Ltd, Gateshead, Tyne & Wear

ACKNOWLEDGEMENTS

This book has taken three years to write and I hope, most sincerely, that I have not forgotten to name any of the people who have been so kind in helping me along the way.

Firstly my deepest thanks to Avril Gray, Brian Pugh and Anne Maclean at Scottish Cultural Press. Also to Gordon Ross Thomson for once more allowing me to use his beautiful and imaginative photographs to illustrate my book. Other photographs came from various sources, and I am grateful to the monks of Pluscarden Abbey, in particular to Father Giles Conacher, who gave much valuable advice as well as images, and to Brother Michael and Brother Benedict.

I also owe a sincere thanks to my friends of many years, Libbie Torrie, Philippa Mather, Alan Leslie-Melville and Jamie Troughton, who have all contributed in various ways.

Elinor Harris, Head of Local Studies in the Headquarters of Argyll & Bute Public Library, Dunoon, went to enormous trouble to root out reference books for which I am very grateful. My thanks also go to Murdo MacDonald, Archivist of Argyll & Bute Council; Margaret Wilson of the Picture Gallery, National Museum of Scotland; Sarah Jane Gibbon, Archive Assistant, Orkney Library & Archives; Mary Wood and Elliot

Rudie, Strathnaver Museum volunteers;
Margaret Urquhart and Estelle Quick of the
Tain & District Museum Trust; Mrs Jean
Ferguson, of Bowmore, Islay, for allowing me
to reproduce her picture of the Pilgrim's
Journey while on loan to the Round Church,
Bowmore; the Revd. Paul Reid, Minister of
the Round Church, and to Graham Dunbar,
who kindly photographed the image and put
it on to a disc. Thanks also to Alan Cameron
and his colleagues at Scotsys, Bellshill, who
painstakingly restored my computer after it
was damaged by lightning.

Lastly, my heart-felt appreciation goes to
my family who give me unfailing support.

When compiling this book, I decided to
divide it into topographical sections, rather
than ordering it chronologically or even
alphabetically.

The main reason is that the dates of some
of the early Christian saints and other
characters involved are, in many cases, so
vague that it is virtually impossible to put
them in strictly sequential order.

Also, for much the same reason, listing the
saints from A to Z would have caused even
greater confusion in relation to historical
periods. Thus, if the story is confined to
regions, I hope that the reader will find it
much easier to trace the pilgrims' routes and
perhaps visit the places associated with the
lives of the saints.

CONTENTS

4

SHRINES OF THE FORTH VALLEY & TAY

5

HEALING WELLS 139

6

ONWARDS TO THE GREAT ABBEYS & CATHEDRALS 149

SACRED TREASURES OF THE ISLES . . 189

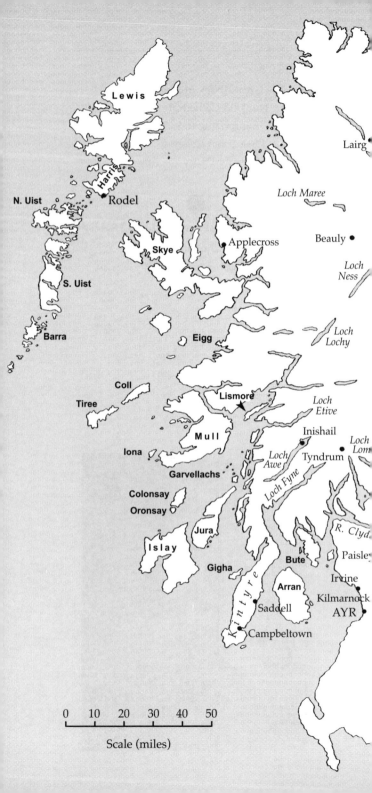

Lewis

Harris

Rodel

N. Uist

S. Uist

Barra

Skye

Applecross

Eigg

Coll

Tiree

Lismore

Mull

Iona

Garvellachs

Colonsay

Oronsay

Jura

Islay

Gigha

Kintyre

Saddell

Campbeltown

Lairg

Loch Maree

Beauly

Loch Ness

Loch Lochy

Loch Etive

Inishail

Loch Awe

Tyndrum

Loch Lom

Loch Fyne

R. Clyde

Paisley

Bute

Arran

Irvine

Kilmarnock

AYR

0   10   20   30   40   50

Scale (miles)

Egilsay

Kirkwall

Orkney Islands

Skail

Tain

Elgin

Banff

Pluscarden

INVERNESS

Culloden

Kingussie

ABERDEEN

Inverbervie

Montrose

North Sea

Dunkeld

Loch Tay

Scone

DUNDEE

Firth of Tay

PERTH

St Andrews

Loch Earn

Cupar

Dunblane

Loch Leven

St Monan's

Isle of May

Dunfermline

Firth of Forth

North Berwick

STIRLING

Whitekirk

Bass Rock

Linlithgow

Haddington

Old Kilpatrick

EDINBURGH

GLASGOW

Queensferry

Newbattle

Soutra

Lanark

Melrose

Roxburgh

Peebles

Dryburgh

Jedburgh

Selkirk

Dumfries

ENGLAND

Wigtown

Kirkcudbright

Whithorn

Isle of Whithorn

The Pilgrim's Journey
to the Celestial City

INTRODUCTION

Pilgrimage . . . A rough road, long and tortuous, springs vividly to mind. One pictures the figures struggling up it towards their unseen destination over the hill. A cripple leaning on his staff, a woman clasping a sick child within her shawl, a company of knights riding gaily yet glancing over their shoulders for the way is beset with danger. Robbers haunt the pilgrim trails. Amongst the horsemen is a young man, lean and hawk-eyed as the bird on his wrist. He sits his palfrey easily as it snatches at the bit. The others pay him deference. His manner betokens him a king . . .

The sun sinks for it is evening. Sparks fly as the iron-shod hooves of the horses strike rough stones on the track. The sound fades into silence. Darkness spreads across the moor . . . A star shines low in the western sky, first a mere suggestion, then brilliant in oncoming frost. A faint noise, barely perceptible, breaks the silence of the night. It grows louder and recognisable as the ringing of a bell. A hooded figure shuffles from nowhere picking its way along the path. It moves furtively and would be unrecognised save for its ringing of the bell. No one follows in its footsteps for this is an outcast, a leper who must travel alone.

What inspired the idea of pilgrimage? Was it because life itself represented a journey to the early Christians? The Celtic and Pictish missionaries emulated the Apostles, to the point where some became martyrs, like the patron saint of pilgrims, St James the Great. The saints themselves were pilgrims – and thus the largely legendary stories of their lives are integral to the development of the quest for redemption which was of such vital importance to the people of Pre-Reformation times.

The search for a deity is something inherent in man. The belief that a cure for mental and physical illness evolved from the pagan conviction that water had magical properties. As Christianity became established in Britain, old superstitions merged with the new faith. Water blessed by the holy men, who understood the mysteries of controlling the elements of the earth, was believed to have extra healing power. The new doctrine also taught that sins, however heinous, could be pardoned by paying tribute to the shrine of a saint. Hardship and exhaustion were essential to procure results. The farther the walk, the more tortuous and dangerous the way, the greater was the chance that the suppliant would find his or her heart's desire . . .

'Some of the greatest wisdom comes from stories'
– Rabbi Blue –

TRAVELLERS FROM BEYOND THE SEAS

P eople of the Celtic race, who came from a settlement on the shores of Lake Neuchâtel, Switzerland, are believed to have brought the culture known as 'La Tène' to Scotland and to Ireland as early as 250BC.

A glance at the map of Europe shows that Lake Neuchâtel drains into the north-flowing River Rhine. The Danube rises east of the watershed: the Saone to the south and the Marne to the east. Thus the origins of La Tène stood in the hub of Europe.

Travellers coming up the Danube brought materials and objects patterned with the designs of Mediterranean countries and beyond. Outstanding amongst the motifs, derived from Greek art, were the palmette, copied from the intricately entwined tendrils of honeysuckle. The boat-shaped pattern of the flower heads resemble the bills of shovellers, wading birds common to the shores of European seas. Also came eastern animal designs of Scythian and other races in the Greek settlements round the Black Sea.

Egypt, south of the Mediterranean, was the source of lattice work, inspired by the plaiting of osiers to form baskets like that in which the infant Moses was found among the rushes of the Nile. The Egyptians themselves are believed to have copied the motifs on goods brought into the Red Sea by vessels from far eastern lands.

The inspiration of those early Celtic craftsmen thus came from far and wide. Some of the ideas were brought into Britain by settlers who, during the years of the Roman occupation, came largely from France. The Romans were recalled to their own country around AD410. They left behind a vacuum of power in which much of their civilisation was destroyed by warring tribes.

Across the sea in Ireland, Christianity was gaining ground to the extent that, in AD431, Pope Celestine I despatched a bishop called Palladius, to organise their church. The work of Palladius was extended by St Patrick and still later by St Finnian who founded the great monastery of Clonard, said to have housed no less than 3,000 monks.

From Clonard, went the missionaries called the Twelve Apostles of Ireland. Among them were two men called Ciaran, one of whom later founded the monastery of Saighir in Munster, and the other, called *Mac-an-Tsaor* 'son of the artificer' who established the even more famous religious house of Clonmacnois, in AD548.

Some 40 years later, in AD590, the church-men of Gaul (then comprising most of France) were astonished by the arrival of a small band of Irish missionaries on their shores. This time they numbered 13 – a leader and 12 followers. Their outer appearance was striking. They wore a garment of coarse texture, woven from wool of the natural colour of the material, with a white tunic underneath. In addition to this they were tonsured in a totally different way to the Gaulish ecclesiastics, their heads being shaven in front from ear to ear. Their foreheads were thus bare while their hair flowed freely at the back. Each man carried a pilgrim's staff, a leathern water-bottle and a wallet, together with a case containing some relics. They spoke amongst themselves in a foreign language, resembling, so the Gauls thought, the dialect of Amorica (the ancient name for Brittany). Nonetheless, conversation was possible because they were fluent in Latin.

When asked who they were and whence they came, they replied 'We are Irish, dwelling at the very ends of the earth.' They then explained themselves to be 'men who receive naught beyond the doctrine of the evangelists and the apostles: the Catholic faith, as it was first delivered by the followers of the holy apostles is still maintained among us with unchanged fidelity.' Their leader, Columbanus, a man of commanding presence and powerful eloquence, then told his listeners, 'I am a Scottish pilgrim and my speech and actions correspond to my name which is in Hebrew *Jonah*, in Greek *Peristera*, and in Latin *Columba* – a dove.'

This forceful personality soon got permission from the local chiefs of the Franks and the Burgundians to build monasteries. Subsequently two establishments, those of Luxeuil and Fontaines, were built in 'recesses' of the Vosges mountains to which 'the youth of the country flocked in numbers for instruction or for training as monks'.

So we have the first description of pilgrims, travelling from Ireland to the Continent, wearing what has come to be recognised as their traditional garb.[1]

Doubtless, they returned to Ireland, bringing with them designs which had come from Mediterranean countries and mythical eastern lands.

Columbanus set out on his mission to Gaul at a time when Irish, or Scottish, settlers, were already established in mainland Argyll. The proximity of Kintyre to Ireland – only 14 miles across the sea – brought many monks to its shores. Some became anchorites, seeking the life of a recluse. Such a one was St Ciaran, who dwelt in a cave on Auchinhoan headland on the south-east point of Kintyre.

Legend has it that St Ciaran himself carved a marigold on a rock within the cave, indeed, the R.C.A.H.M.S. (Royal Commission on the Ancient and Historical Monuments of Scotland) states that 'the cave is traditionally associated with St Ciaran, Abbot of

Clonmacnois.' Similar marigold patterns 'made by the play of compasses within circles, are found on Early Christian stones and metalwork in Ireland, the Isle of Man and Scotland at dates ranging from the 7th to the 12th century. The tips of the six-petal flower, linked by arcs, are enclosed within a circular T-fret border which, like the marigold itself, appears on Pictish silver bowls found on St Ninian's Isle in Shetland dated around AD800.'[2]

This is one of the first examples of Early Christian sculpture in Scotland which proves the importation of Celtic patterns from Europe that was taking place at that time. The marigold, emblem of the rays of light, grows freely in Mediterranean countries. Is it therefore safe to assume that the carving was made by a monk – in all probability a hermit – who dreamed of the warmth of sunshine as he laboured to create an effigy of the flower of the golden rays? Perhaps, as he rested, stretching his aching back, he glanced out at the sea, which at high tide reaches almost to the mouth of the cave. Gulls, screaming on the mist born wind, must have been his only companions, except perhaps for seals. Engulfed in cold, damp and isolation, he dreamt of blue water and sand, golden as the flower which he chiselled with so much dexterity upon the surface of the rock.

EARLY CHRISTIAN CROSSES

By the middle of the 5th century, churchmen from Ireland were travelling to the Continent in ever increasing numbers. It cannot therefore be mere coincidence that the sculptors in the Irish monasteries began increasingly to use designs which incorporate those on monumental carvings in European countries, linked by the great trading route of the River Danube to the Black Sea and beyond.

The first Early Christian crosses in Scotland were crude efforts of workmanship compared to those in Ireland created at a similar date. They may, in fact, have been made as a compromise by local people, who, imbibed with superstition and unconvinced by the Christian missionaries, clung to the old pagan beliefs. Cross-decorated slabs, which commonly take the form of four bosses standing within circular hollows, may have been partly developed from the cup and ring marks of the Pre-Christian Age, which abound throughout Scotland, particularly in the north-west Highlands and the Isles.

During the 8th century, in the great monastic houses of Ireland, the expertise of masons was reaching a state of perfection hitherto unknown. Churchmen returning from the Continent brought with them designs, which sculptors copied on blocks of stone.

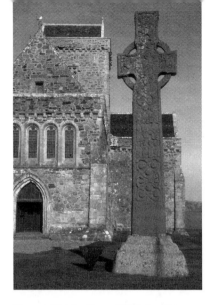

The early Christian Cross of St Martin which stands to the west of the Abbey Church, Iona

Craftsmen were also being sent from Ireland to Iona, probably at the requests of the abbots who, as administrators of Columba's abbey, controlled what had now become the great religious centre of the Isles.

The four free-standing crosses on Iona – St John's, St Martin's, St Matthew's and St Oran's – together with those in the churchyard of the Old Parish Church of Kildalton in Islay, must be the greatest treasures in Scotland of Early Christian art. Of the quartet on Iona only St Martin's, thought to be the latest and dated from about the middle to the end of the 8th century, survives in the entirety of its original form. The cross still stands on its original base, deeply rooted in the ground. It is carved from a single block

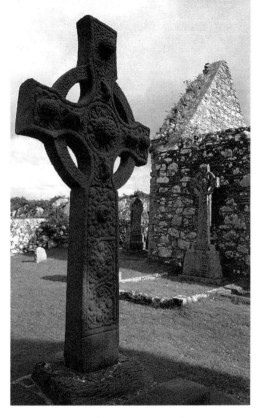

Kildalton Cross, Islay. One of the most beautiful early
Christian crosses, thought to date from the 8th century

of grey-green epidiorite, probably brought in
by boat from the Argyll mainland, so durable
that it has resisted the onslaught of the
elements for at least 1,400 years.

The cross-head, on the east side, is
designed around five bosses. Below on the
shaft, 24 serpents intertwine round three
circular groups of cruciform bosses, smaller
than those above. The west side shows
groups of biblical figures. Firstly, at the

bottom of the shaft, a man with right arm raised, is taken to be Samuel anointing David with oil. David with his musicians, one playing a harp, another a wind instrument, are above. Higher still, Abraham sacrifices Isaac, while at the top of the shaft a man flanked by beasts, appears to be Daniel and the lions. The centre of the cross-head itself shows the Virgin and Child surrounded by four little angels one sheltering their heads with his wing. To left and right on the side-arms two fierce lion-like animals, face each other, tufted tails curling over their backs, while above them, on the top arm, three pairs of sleeping lions, their tails entwined, lie back to back.[3]

On Islay, the Kildalton Cross, likewise thought to date from the 8th century, bears so much resemblance to the Iona crosses that it is taken to be the work of a mason brought specifically from that island. Again, it is carved from a single slab of grey-green epidiorote, in this case the local stone not, as in Iona, imported from elsewhere. Most noticeably the creatures depicted here are inspired by travellers' tales. On the shaft of the west face serpents – unknown in Ireland – surround bosses in a circular form. Four lions ornament the cross-head above. On the left of the reverse side, Cain is slaying Abel with the jaw-bone of an ass. On the right, Abraham is preparing to make a sacrifice of Isaac, much as is depicted on St Martin's Cross in Iona. At the top of the shaft, the Virgin and Child are surrounded by angels is an almost exact replica of the carving on St Oran's Cross.[4]

These crosses remain in proof of the first great period of sculpture created in the Inner Hebrides by masons who came from Ireland to Iona.

Alas, it was all too soon to end. By the middle of the 9th century, Vikings, based in Orkney, were sailing their longships ever farther south. Thirsting for destruction, they slew the monks on Iona, before bursting into the abbey to steal and destroy all they could find. Those who survived are believed to have rescued the famous *Book of Kells*, taking it from Iona to Kells in Co Meath, Ireland (it now rests in Trinity College, Dublin).

Iona Cathedral, built on the site of
St Columba's Chapel of the 6th century

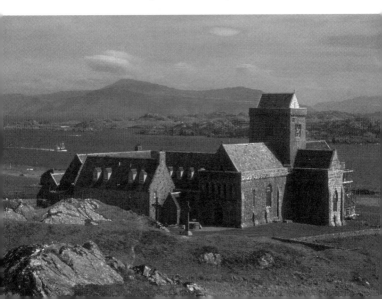

Then followed a period, lasting 300 years, when the wood and wattle buildings of the early monastic settlements were largely burnt to the ground. All that was moveable was taken, or else wantonly shattered.

Fortunately, however, stone is durable. Also, due to its weight, it is difficult to move. Thus, some of the mighty crosses, magnificent both in beauty and symmetry of design, survive as examples of the Romanesque art.

Brought first to Ireland, and from there to Iona, by clerics travelling to and from the monastic houses of Europe, the designs descend from the age when Christianity was spreading through the western sphere.

THE PILGRIMS' ROUTE TO IONA

St Oran, an Irish evangelist believed to have reached Iona before Columba, gave his name to an almost square piece of ground adjoining the Cathedral where, according to tradition, lie the remains of 60 kings – 48 of them Scottish, the rest Irish and Norwegian – as well as many churchmen and clan chiefs. The last of the Scottish kings to be buried in the Reilig Oran (crypt of Oran) was Donald III (Donald bàn) who died in 1097.

Tradition dictated that their bodies were carried across land and over water, along the

pilgrims' route. A glance at the Ordnance
Survey Map shows how the old tracks,
marked by dotted lines, were connected by
rivers and lochs. From east and central
Scotland, a direct route lay up the River Tay,
along Loch Tay, through Glen Dochart and
Strathfillan, and then down Glen Lochy and
Glen Orchy to Loch Awe. From there, the
road to the Isles, the 'Streng of Lorn' runs
across the hills from Loch Avich to Loch
Feochan, an inlet of the Firth of Lorn. Here,
near Kilninver, on the south side of the loch,
coffins were shipped from Creag na Marbh
('Rock of the Dead') to be taken across to
Mull.

They were landed at Port nam Marbh, a
place almost opposite the rock in Loch
Feochan, on the north side of the narrow
entrance to the deep-water harbour of Loch
Spelve on the east coast of Mull. From the
landing place, the coffins were carried on
spokes (two long pieces of wood) along a
rough track round the loch. The path led past
the now almost totally ruined church of
Killean, the Old Parish Church, dedicated to
St John, first recorded in 1393 when a Papal
Indulgence (a pardon from the temporal
punishment of a sin), was granted to pilgrims
who visited and made donations of food and
wine.[5]

Leaving the shore, the funeral corteges
made their way – with many pauses for
refreshment during which the coffins were
laid upon flattened rocks – to join an ancient

route from east to west across the south part of Mull. Later, this became a drover's road.

Starting at Grass Point (the landing and departure point for the cattle on the east shore of the Sound of Mull), it follows the same line of the present-day mostly single-track road. Beside the River Lussa ('river of the herbs') the road rises gently upwards through Glen More, then descends beside the River Colada ('river of the poppies') to the sea. Onwards from the bridge across the Allt Teanga ('water of the tongues') the way is marked by standing stones, each incised with a cross, along the south shore of Loch Scridain to the little village of Fionnphort, which lies just beyond the last of the stones.

This is the place where, from time immemorial, boats have plied back and forth across the Sound of Iona, carrying pilgrims to the little island in the Atlantic on which St Columba came ashore so many years ago.

Standing stone, just outside Fionnphort

ALL ROADS
LEAD TO ROME

S o the old saying goes, yet the converse was true during the first 400 years of the first millennium AD.

Having landed at Dover in 50BC, Julius Caesar reached inland as far as the Thames. Nearly a century later, in AD43, a force said to number 70,000 men, commanded by Aulus Plautius, began the colonisation of England. The Britons, led by Boadicea, failed to defeat them and, by AD78, the country as far north as York, together with a large part of Wales, were part of the vast Roman Empire.

Gnaeus Julius Agricola became governor of the conquered colony. He invaded Scotland – then called Caledonia – and first subdued the Borders and the Lothians before heading into Ayrshire in AD82.

In AD83, probably on the orders of the new emperor Domitian, he advanced north as far as Aberdeenshire. In AD84, he began his most successful campaign, which culminated at the unidentified place of Mons Grapius (thought to have been in Perthshire or Angus) when the Pictish King Galgacus attacked with a large force. Many on both sides were killed. But this desperate stand by the native Scottish people resulted in victory for the invaders.

Agricola withdrew his army to forts in the great central valley of the rivers Clyde and Forth. Shortly afterwards he ordered his fleet to sail round Scotland. His sailors, discovering the Orkneys, annexed them to the Roman Empire. However, despite the extent of his triumphs, or because the Emperor Domitian was jealous of his success, Agricola was then recalled to Rome.

The Scottish tribes attacked the Roman settlements with increasing ferocity until the Emperor Hadrian came to Britain himself. He at once realised the necessity of building a line of defences strong enough to repel attack. Thus five years later, in AD122, the building of the massive Hadrian's Wall began. Stretching from Bowness, on the Solway, to Wallsend, on the Tyne – a distance of 73 miles – it defined the northern boundary of Roman Britain.

The wall was one of the most amazing creations of architecture ever seen. Nonetheless, following the death of Hadrian, Scottish tribes broke through and raided the north of England. Subsequently Antoninus Pius, the Emperor who succeeded Hadrian in AD138, sent Q. Lollius Urbicus to Scotland. He built the Antonine Wall, which stretched for 36 miles between Old Kilpatrick, in the Firth of Clyde, and Bridgeness on the Forth. Urbicus is believed to have driven the people called Brigantes from their territory between the Humber and the Forth beyond this fortification and into the land of the Picts, described as a kindred race.

The lifestyle of the Romans differed greatly from that of the people who dwelt in the vicinity of their camps. Nonetheless, as inevitably happens with armies of occupation, many of the soldiers integrated with the local population amongst whom they found concubines and in some cases perhaps even wives. Gradually, they accepted Roman ways of behaviour and assimilated some of their beliefs.

Christianity was, almost certainly, introduced into Britain during the Roman occupation. However, the Roman soldiers, who came from many parts of Europe, as well as from the Middle East, were not entirely Christian. Many worshipped the Roman gods, in particular Mithra, slayer of the Sacred Bull. Those Britons persecuted for their religion in England, probably took refuge amongst the Picts living north of the Antonine Wall. It was not until AD306 that Constantine, the first Christian Roman Emperor, granted freedom of conscience to all Christians. In AD314, following the Edict of Milan of AD312, Constantine summoned a Council at Arles, to which no less than three bishops from Britain came. Foremost amongst their decisions was the acceptance of the Roman date for Easter, which became the rule of the British and Irish and, later, the Columban churches.

The Council of Nicaea in AD325 greatly influenced the faith of Christians in Scotland. Athanasius, who attended, was a passionate

believer in the full divinity of Christ. He
imparted his zeal for the Nicene Creed to
Hilary of Poitiers (Bishop of Poitiers,
AD353–367), who in turn moulded the belief
of St Martin of Tours. The treatise *De Synodis*,
composed by Hilary, includes a reference to
the orthodoxy of the bishops of the province
of Britain. In Scotland, the fame of Hilary
spread as far north as Shetland where
'St Hilary's Kirk' once stood in the parish of
Fetlar and North Yell.

During the 4th century, the Romans
continued the great network of building
throughout Britain. The Viae, the great road
that ran from London to York and Carlisle,
continued west to Galloway and north to the
Antonine Wall. Travelling was easy. The roads
were constantly repaired. Bridges were made
over rivers. Inns gave accommodation and
horses could be had for hire.

Nonetheless, despite these benefits,
opposition to the Roman occupation steadily
increased. In AD343 the Picts and the Scots of
Ulster made a combined attack. Their
numbers included a mysterious tribe of
people called 'Attacotti', known to be
cannibals, who may have adhered to either
side. United, they broke through Hadrian's
Wall and devastated the north of England.
Constans, son of Constantine, subdued them,
but after his death, they attacked again.

The fighting continued for nearly 20 years.
The Picts and Scots killed and burned nearly
as far south as London and it seemed as

though the Romans must be overcome. But in AD369 the Emperor Valentinian I sent Theodosius the Elder to save the Roman colony. The Picts were driven back behind the Antonine Wall. The Scots eventually fled across the Irish Channel to their homeland and some of the bestial Attacotti, forced into the Roman levie, ended up in Gaul.

Thus, Roman authority in Britain was restored. But within 30 years Rome itself was threatened by invading hordes. The legions were summoned back and Hadrian's Wall was abandoned *circa* AD400. The Romans who had ruled England and much of Scotland for nearly four centuries were at last leaving British shores. They left behind a country made accessible by long straight roads.

The idea of pilgrimage sprang largely from the Crusades (which began in 1095). The Crusaders who went to Spain to fight the Saracens were amazed by the architectural beauty of the cathedrals of France and Spain. In particular, they admired the Romanesque cathedral of Compostella, built in 1078. The cathedral is said to stand above the underground shrine which contains the relics of the apostle St James.

According to tradition, the remains of the saint, after he was executed by a sword, were miraculously conveyed to Spain. From the 13th century Spanish artists have depicted St James as a pilgrim wearing a cloak with a long cape, a scallop-shell on his shoulder or on his lapped hat, and leaning on the long staff from which hangs his gourd of water.

The scallop-shell is particularly associated with St James because the legend runs that the vessel carrying his remains to Spain rescued a horse and rider from drowning. Interestingly, the bodies of both were said to be covered with scallop-shells. The beaches of Galicia abound in these shells, which proved a fruitful source of income to the custodians of the apostle's shrine.

Pilgrims to the shrine of Compostella were so frequently attacked by the Moors that hospitals were erected for them at different places along the route by the monks of St Helie, 'which might serve for house-room and lodgings to the said pilgrims of St James, to help and heal them in the case of sickness or other distresses'.

A small jet figure about 13cm (five inches) high, presented to the Museum of National Antiquities in Edinburgh in about 1885, was found to be a Signaculum of St James of Compostella, which had probably been worn by a leprous pilgrim to that famous shrine.

Pilgrimages to Compostella from Scotland were not uncommon in the Middle Ages due to the fact that the pilgrim's house and property were 'in the king's peace' (under royal protection) until he returned home.[1]

The Knights Templar was another outcome of the Crusades, having been formed to protect pilgrims travelling to the Holy Land. Their military order was founded c.1118 to guard the converging roads to the Holy Sepulchre at Jerusalem and the shrine itself. They were brought to Scotland by King David I (1124–53) as his spiritual advisors.

The Hospitallers, or Knights of St John, founded c.1090 by philanthropic merchants of Amalfi to give aid to sick pilgrims in Jerusalem, were also introduced to Scotland during David's reign. Their chief house in Scotland was the preceptory of Torphichen, in West Lothian, which became a place of sanctuary for pilgrims and people in need.

The Hospitallers had lands in different parts of the country which were in some cases shared with the Templars who came in increasing numbers to Scotland after the suppression of their order by Henry II of France in 1312. Robert the Bruce encouraged

Legend has it that St Anthony's Chapel, Holyrood Park, Edinburgh, was built as an annex for the knightly order of St Anthony, or Knights Templar, and it soon became a place of pilgrimage (see page 145)

them to settle and some historians assert that a contingent of their order fought for him on the field of Bannockburn in 1314.

Bruce had been excommunicated by Pope Clement V for his murder of the 'Red Comyn' before the altar of Greyfriars Abbey in Dumfries. Pardoned after many years, he clung to his great ambition to make a pilgrimage against the infidels who defied Christian beliefs. On his death-bed, he entrusted Sir James Douglas to carry his embalmed heart on a crusade against the Saracens in Spain.

In medieval Scotland, as elsewhere in Europe, pilgrims sought the shrines of saints. It was only after the Protestant Reformation of 1560, when the worship of relics was declared to be idolatry, that the long established search for redemption was prohibited by the Kirk.

ST NINIAN

The Man Who Trod the Roman Roads

The birth date of the Scottish boy who became St Ninian is a matter of controversy among scholars. Originally, he was thought to have been born about AD362, at the time when the Picts from Scotland and Scots from Ulster were ravaging the land under Roman rule. Ninian's father is said to have been the chief of a tribe that held land on both sides of the Solway Firth.

Archaeological research has shown that people at that time, in terror of the Pictish and Irish invaders, were living in caves.

The two main authorities for Ninian's life are the Venerable Bede, who wrote at Jarrow during AD673–735 (over 200 years after what he thought to be the date of Ninian's death) and Ailred of Rievaulx, whose *Life of Ninian* was written in the 12th century. Ailred states categorically that Ninian was an 'adolescens' (adolescent) when he went to Rome.

Taking the date of Ninian's birth to be AD362, he would have been about seven when Theodosius arrived to restore authority within the Roman colony in Britain. Therefore he could, as is claimed, have travelled to Rome once peace was restored.

If, on the other hand, he was born later, towards the end of the 5th century, as some historians believe, he would have reached the Continent along roads which, by then, had become relics of the Roman occupation.

Conditions in Europe at that time would not have been easy. Civilisation in Italy collapsed after Rome was captured by the Visigoths in AD410. Vandals swarmed in from Africa. In AD450, Attila caused widespread devastation in both Italy and France and order was only restored to both countries towards the end of the 5th century.

On his journey, Ninian must have followed the Roman Road to London and Sandwich, then crossed the English Channel, found his way through Gaul, crossed the

Gallician Alps by Mont Genève, descended into Italy and thus reached Rome. Dr Frank Knight, who mapped out this route, believed that he reached the Papal city in about AD377.

Travellers were certainly going back and forth from Scotland to Europe by that time. During excavations at Whithorn, in Galloway, a few pieces of reddish wheelmade pottery were discovered and were proved to have come from the east Mediterranean, or the Greek Isles of the Aegean.[2]

How long Ninian stayed in Rome is unknown, but both early accounts agree that he returned to Scotland through Tours where he met and was instructed by St Martin, the soldier turned monk, whose beliefs had been largely moulded by Hilary of Poitiers.

Of course, if Ninian travelled at a much later date, he could not have actually met Martin who died *circa* AD398. Nonetheless, he would have assimilated his doctrines of self-denial and belief that administration to the poor and sick was essential to the will of God.

Early accounts state that Ninian, on leaving Tours, asked St Martin if he could take two masons back to Scotland. Once returned to Galloway, again according to Ailred, 'a great multitude went out to meet him; there was great joy among all; and the praise of God sounded on all sides'. This must signify that the people of Galloway were already Christian, having accepted the faith of the Romans who colonised their land.

Ninian turned his attention to converting

the Southern Picts, centred around Stirling in the valley of the Forth, who still worshipped heathen gods. In his time, the journey from Galloway to the Forth could be made largely on the Roman roads. Recent research suggests that a very early church existed at St Ninian's in Stirling. Also, a medieval biographer of St Kentigern (patron saint of Glasgow), claims that a burial site at Cadder, on the Antonine Wall, was consecrated by St Ninian.[3]

Once returned to Galloway, Ninian had his French masons construct a church of stone washed with white lime. Local people were astonished, Scottish churches having hitherto been made of wood. Candida Casa ('the white house') gleamed like a beacon of faith. Ailred says that it stood on 'Witerna, which, situated on the shore of the ocean, and extending far into the sea on the east, west and south sides, is closed in by the sea itself, while only on the north is the way open to those who would enter.'

The ruins of the Priory nave at Whithorn
(by kind permission of the Whithorn Trust)

Ailred seems to be referring to the 13th-century chapel on the Isle of Whithorn. This is where pilgrims, from as far away as France, came ashore. In fact, the town of Witerna is the modern-day Whithorn, three miles inland, and Candida Casa is believed to have been sited on top of the hill in Whithorn where successive churches have been built.

From the island (now connected to the mainland by a short permanent causeway), pilgrims would have made their way to this hill in Whithorn to visit St Ninian's Priory Church. This stood at the eastern end of the crypt of the cathedral, founded by Fergus, Lord of Galloway, in 1186.

Excavations during the 1950s revealed an early Christian stone church at the east end of this cathedral, which had been painted with 'a course cream mortar of poor quality'.

The medieval cathedral became the shrine to St Ninian to which pilgrims flocked in their hundreds for over 400 years. They included men and women of all ages and from all walks of life, as Ailred states:

> *When the blessed Ninian had been translated into the Heavens, the faithful people who had loved him in life, frequented with the greatest devotion that which seemed to them all that was left of him, namely his most holy relics.*

Robert the Bruce made a pilgrimage to Whithorn just before he died, apparently of leprosy, in 1329. So many followed him that, during their successive reigns, the Regent Albany and then his nephew, James I, decreed that safe conduct be granted to all pilgrims.

In 1473, James III and his Scandinavian Queen Margaret made at least two pilgrimages to Whithorn but it was their son, James IV, who came so often that the fame of the little town grew.

The Lord Treasurer's Account, which gives details of his fairly lavish spending, also describes his routes, sometimes down the west coast through Ayrshire, sometimes through Lanarkshire or Kirkcudbright. A favourite lodging was Tongland Abbey on the Dee, three miles north of Kirkcudbright. In Galloway itself the king often stayed at Glenluce Abbey, Wigtown Friary or the priory at Whithorn. In 1508, on the way from Edinburgh to Biggar, the royal entourage was joined by four Italian minstrels who, insisting on being provided with horses, caused great extra expense.[4]

An arm bone, most precious relic of St Ninian, by then disintegrating, was encased in silver by King James. Kept at Whithorn until the time of the Reformation, it was then taken to France, only to be lost in the turmoil of the Revolution.

In *Wild Men and Holy Places*, Daphne Brooke brings the royal pilgrimages vividly to mind. She describes how the popular king and his queen (if she was with him) proceeded through the streets before they

Wood carving of a bishop found near Whithorn, and thus thought to be St Ninian (courtesy of the National Museum of Scotland)

entered the cathedral where hundreds of candles burned. 'The bishop with his gilded crosier,[5] accompanied by the mitred prior, led the royal party, then followed the white-clad canons and the chanting choir, and after them nobles, gentry, burgesses and a host of pilgrims. Inside the cathedral the king was led to the High Altar, to the Lady Chapel, to the Rood Altar and into the crypt. There were the tomb and relics – the shrine – lit by wax candles that were never allowed to fail.'

Royal pilgrimages, however, were not always attended with magnificence. In 1507, James IV walked barefoot to Whithorn when his wife, Margaret Tudor, was thought to be dying. After she had miraculously recovered, they returned together on horseback to give thanks to St Ninian.

Their son, James V, also made a pilgrimage to Whithorn as did his daughter, Mary Queen of Scots. By the time of her visit in 1563, the Kirk, under the influence of John Knox, was violently opposed to pilgrimages, seen as a form of idolatry by the Presbyterian Church. An Act of Parliament was passed to prohibit them in 1581. Nevertheless, here as elsewhere in Scotland, people still came secretly to the shrines of the saints.

Today, in the Whithorn Museum, visitors can see the famous carved pillar stone which was found during 19th-century excavations. Known as the Latimer Stone and believed to be the earliest Christian memorial in Scotland, it may have been carved about 1,600 years ago when St Ninian came to Galloway to spread the word of God.

The spread of Christianity in Scotland

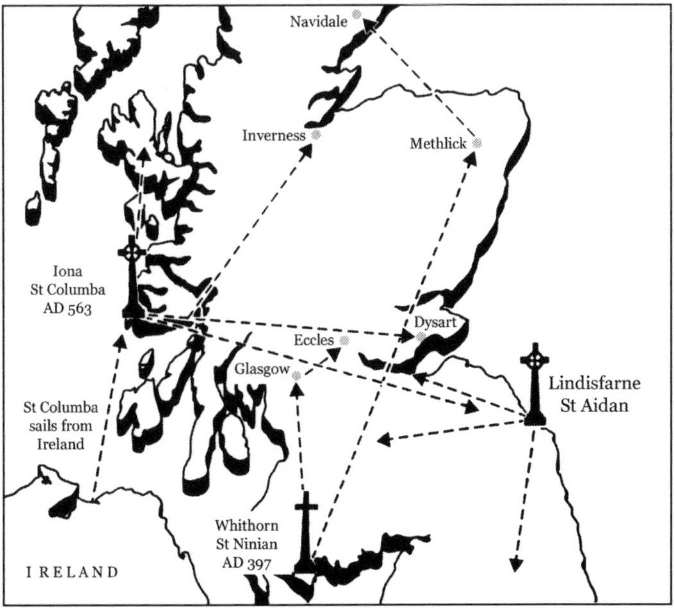

Navidale

Inverness

Methlick

Iona
St Columba
AD 563

Eccles

Dysart

Glasgow

Lindisfarne
St Aidan

St Columba
sails from
Ireland

Whithorn
St Ninian
AD 397

IRELAND

Pilgrims of the River Clyde

The estuary of the River Clyde has been used by boats going to and from the east coast of Ireland from before recorded time. In the troubled years following the Roman evacuation of Britain, bands of pirates from Ireland frequently raided the Scottish coast.

St Patrick
Patron Saint of Ireland

A legend runs that sometime around the year AD430, a boy who was fishing from a rock in the Clyde was seized by a gang of these brigands and carried off as a captive to become a slave in Ireland.

This cannot be substantiated, but many biographers of St Patrick claim that he came from a land-owning family of Britons (who were Christians), that he had been born in the parish of Kilpatrick, near Dumbarton Rock, and that he had actually been a slave in Ireland. Patrick eventually escaped from slavery in Ireland, walked to the coast and managed to find a ship to take him back to Scotland.[1] His family begged him to remain with them but in a vision he heard the voice of Irish people imploring him to come back and live with them.

Convinced that he had found his true vocation, he trained as a priest, became ordained as a bishop and then set sail for Ireland – the country of his former captivity. He describes in his own *Confessio* how he struggled to become a missionary, a task in which he was ultimately successful. He died there on 17 March 493.

St Patrick is essentially Irish and for that reason Kilpatrick, believed to be the place of his birth, became a place of pilgrimage until the time of the Reformation *c.*1560. Many pilgrims came in search of St Patrick's Stone, a rock in the Clyde (opposite the parish church of Old Kilpatrick), from which, according to local tradition, he was captured by the pirates.[2] A well, now long vanished, in which he is said to have been baptised was also a popular place of pilgrimage. So many came that a 'hospital' had to be built to house them beside the church. Most would have arrived by boat, the easiest way to travel, but Highland folk would most likely have come up the Blane valley and from thence followed the footpaths over the Kilpatrick hills.

The Clyde was then much shallower (it was dredged from the 18th century onwards to allow steamers to reach the Broomielaw) and, particularly in dry weather, people coming from the south could have waded or ridden through parts of the stream. The ford at Inchinnan, close to Kilpatrick, must have been on a main route. Thus, for nearly 1,000 years, the traditional birthplace of St Patrick, patron saint of Ireland, brought pilgrims from near and far.

St Kentigern

Patron Saint of Glasgow

The history of St Kentigern – or St Mungo as he is also known – is shrouded in the mists of time. His first biography, *Historia Beati Kentigerni*, was composed for Bishop Herbert, Bishop of Glasgow from 1147–1164. The second, called *Vita Kentigerni*, was written by a monk, Jocelin of Furness, on the instruction of Bishop Jocelin of Glasgow (1170–1179).[3]

If St Kentigern was a contemporary of St Columba – as both biographies claim him to have been – then these accounts were written nearly 600 years after his death.

The two biographies give slightly different versions of the legend attributed to his birth, but the main points are roughly the same. Leudonus, King of Leudonia (Lothian) was a pagan. His daughter, Thaney, was raped and became pregnant. In a fury, Leodonus ordered that his unfortunate daughter should be placed in a cart and pushed off the top of Traprain Law. Surprisingly, she reached the bottom unharmed whereupon her father had her put into a coracle which was set adrift. The boat carried her via the May Isle to Culross on the Fife shore where she gave birth to her child. Both mother and son were rescued by St Serf and given sanctuary.

The story goes on to tell how the boy was called Kentigern or Mungo, meaning 'darling'. Raised by the saint, Kentigern trained to be a monk. In time, he left Culross and went to a place called 'Kernach' (Carnock, near Airth). Here, he met an old man named Fergus, who promptly expired before his eyes. Placing the body in a cart drawn by two unbroken bullocks, Kentigern took him to 'Glascu' where he buried him in a grove of trees near the church.

After some time, Kentigern was elected bishop by the king and clergy of the Cambrian region, which stretched from 'sea to sea' – presumably across the central valley from the Clyde to the Forth. The wooden church near where Fergus was buried then became the cathedral of the widespread diocese over which Kentigern held control.

Later, Kentigern incurred the wrath of the despotic King Morken of Cambria, who, in a time of famine, refused to let Kentigern take wheat to feed the poor from the royal barns by the Clyde. Undeterred, Kentigern commanded the river to rise in spate and miraculously it conveyed the sheds to

Kentigern's church. Morken, furious, literally kicked out the holy man and was subsequently stricken with gout.

The king died of his affliction, after which Kentigern, warned that the pagans were plotting to kill him, fled Scotland for Wales. Arriving in 553, the legend runs that he was led by a white boar to Llanelwy where he founded a monastery.

During the 20 years that Kentigern is said to have stayed in Wales, Scotland and the north of England were repeatedly attacked by raiders from the Baltic and Friesland. The situation became critical as the invaders threatened to push their way from coast to coast across Britain.

But in 573 an army of Christian tribes defeated a pagan force on the west side of the Esk, some eight miles north of Carlisle. The victorious Christians were descended from the old Romanized Britons who Ninian had converted, and were united under Rydderch Hael, King of Strathclyde, whose capital was Dunbarton.

Jocelin, Kentigern's biographer, says that on hearing of the victory, Kentigern came back to Scotland with no less than 665 monks. Rydderch went to meet him at Hoddam in Dumfriesshire where Kentigern established another religious centre from which he spread the word of God.

After eight years at Hoddam, he returned to his wooden cathedral in Glasgow.

Many miracles followed. Most famous, is

the story connected with Glasgow's coat of arms, which shows a salmon with a ring in its mouth. The ring was a present from King Rydderch to his wife Languoreth. Foolishly, she gave the ring to a young knight with whom she had fallen in love. One day, the king found her paramour asleep, saw the ring, pulled it from his finger and threw it into the River Clyde. He then demanded that his wife show him the ring. Needless to say, she could not produce it, whereupon he had her cast into prison. Desperate to save her life, she begged Kentigern to help her. He sent a man to catch a salmon from the river, presented it to the king and, wonder of wonders, there was the ring inside the fish.

Because of the danger of travelling, when Christians ran the risk of attack from pagan tribesman, few of the monks from St Ninian's foundation of Candida Casa at Whithorn in Galloway were brave enough to go forth as missionaries. Thus, Christianity in the Borders and in Central Scotland had lost much ground. However, thanks to the protection of Rydderch Hael, Kentigern and his monks were able to evangelise throughout the Borders and the centre and east of Scotland. After eight years, however, he returned to Glasgow, his ecclesiastical home.

From there he travelled even farther. Through Fife and over the Ochils to the foot of Gleneagles where a church – still called St Mungo's – stands close to one of the many St Mungo's Wells. Later, he is believed to have journeyed up the east coast to Aberdeenshire where his name is enshrined in churches and again in wells. Intrepid traveller as he was, stories tell of his going as far north as Orkney and the Faröe Islands, although as he got older, his brethren acted in his place.[4]

St Kentigern's meeting with St Columba is said to have taken place near to the Cathedral by the Molendinar burn. The two saints were attended by monks loudly singing psalms. Adomnan, St Columba's first biographer, makes no mention of this. However, since it is generally believed that Columba and Kentigern were contemporaries, the story may have some truth.[5]

St Kentigern is thought to have died in 603 – the same year as King Rydderch Hael – at the great age, especially at that time, of 85. He was buried in Glasgow in the church he founded; his tomb destined to be the goal of pilgrims for many generations to come.

The first stone cathedral in Glasgow was built on the site of St Kentigern's cell – shortly before David I became king in 1124. The church was consecrated in 1136. Later, it was largely destroyed by fire but the foundations are believed to have survived and lie beneath the nave of the present church.

The great rebuilding of the late 12th century was the work of Bishop Jocelin, who commissioned the second biography of St Kentigern by Jocelin of Furness, the scribe who shared his name.

Glasgow Cathedral where the site of Kentigern's shrine, a major venue for pilgrims, can still be seen to this day

The position of the saint's tomb on a slope inspired the layout of the cathedral. The nave was laid out above the grave which lay in the crypt below and thus was constructed an upper and a lower church.

The vaulting of the lower church was cleverly designed to enhance both the position of the tomb of St Kentigern in the middle of the central aisle and that of the altar of the Blessed Virgin, 'Our Lady of Glasgow', at its east end. So many pilgrims came that 'a pilgrim route', reminiscent of a one-way traffic system, was designed round the floor of the crypt.[6]

The fame of St Kentigern, or St Mungo, rests largely on the fact that his biographers, particularly Jocelin of Furness, gave him an identity with which people in medieval times could identify, even as we do today.

St Constantine

The identity of St Constantine is confused. Jocelin of Furness, biographer of St Kentigern, claims that Constantine was a son of King Rhydderch of Glasgow, granted to his queen, Languoreth, in old age in answer to St Kentigern's prayers. The *Breviary* however, asserts that his father was Padarn, or Paternus, king of Cornwall.[7]

Peter Yeoman in his *Pilgrimage in Medieval Scotland* sums it up by saying that 'the precise identity of St Constantine is uncertain; he could be a compilation of the legends of two or three separate holy men of that name, or more likely, he was a dynastic saint of the Scottish royal house, which included a number of Constantines at the end of the 9th century.'[8]

The earlier accounts, which place him in the 6th century, hang largely on the legends transcending from that time.

Whatever his paternity, Constantine is said to have become king of the British province of Cornwall where he committed terrible crimes. His villainy culminated in the murder of the two sons of Modred (son of Loth, the Prince of Lothian) within the precincts of a church. St Gildas rebuked him, begging him to 'Turn thine eyes back . . . and come to Christ.' Moved by these words, or else by sorrow at the death of his wife, thought to be a daughter of the King of Lesser Britain and whom he seems to have greatly loved, Constantine resigned his crown and swore to become a missionary of the Christian faith.

He is claimed to have begun his work as an evangelist in Cornwall, where the parish of Constantine still bears his name. Moving to Wales, he studied in the monastery of St David at Menevia. From there he crossed the sea to Ireland to the monastery of Rathen where he worked as a lay brother grinding corn. Somehow his identity was discovered by the abbot who had him instructed and ordained. Returning across the Irish Sea to Scotland, Constantine sailed up the Clyde to Govan where he founded a monastery of his own.[9]

Acting on the hypothesis that Constantine was a contemporary of St Kentigern in the 6th or early 7th centuries, his choice of a site for a church at Govan was ideal. It was easy to travel up the Clyde Valley and to sail down the estuary of the river to Kintyre. It does, in fact, seem probable that Constantine's church in Govan was originally of more importance than that of Kentigern in Glasgow.[10]

Constantine may have also founded chapels in the south of Scotland. In Kirkcudbright the Chapel of Constantine in Urr parish (now long vanished) bore his name. In Perth, the chapel in Kinnoull parish (given to Cambuskenneth Abbey in the 13th century) was dedicated to Constantine. In

Angus, at Dunnichen, where the church is called 'St Causnan', the Fair of St Causnan was once held every March.

Traditionally, Constantine, who is believed to have lived in the second half of the 6th century, is thought to have been a contemporary of both St Kentigern and St Columba (c.521–97). He may have reached the Western Isles, for at Garrabost, on the Eye Peninsula, near Stornoway, 'St Cowstan's Chapel' stood beside the shore. However, he is best remembered in the south-east corner of Kintyre.

The ruined church of Kilchousland stands above cliffs on the coast about five miles north of Campbeltown. Across the sea lies Arran and the little tidal island of Davarr. The church apparently takes its name from the

Kilchousland Church, near Campbeltown, where
St Constantine was murdered by pirates as he preached

local saint called Couslan[11] but it could be argued to be linked to St Constantine instead as it is here (or somewhere nearby), that he is believed to have died.

Having long wished to become a martyr, Constantine's desire was fulfilled. He was preaching to the local people – we are told they were all within the church – when a party of pirates landed on the shore below. Creeping up unseen they burst into the building and fell upon the congregation.

> They cut off the hand of Constantine's attendant but the saint cured it at a touch. So they raged against the man of God, and afflicted him with various torments; and among other mortal wounds they also cut off his fore-arm. And they went away leaving him for dead. Then the saint called together his brethren, and consoled them in charity . . . And he died about the year of the Lord 576.[12]

Sources which give his death at a later date include Dr G.A. Frank Knight, who believed it to be 11 March 590.

Following his death, Constantine's body was carried by his devoted disciples to be buried in the church he had built in Govan. The church information leaflet gives the date of his burial as 13 July 577.

Govan Parish Church was rebuilt in 1762 and again in 1826. The fourth church on the same site was constructed in 1884–88 on the plans of the architect Robert Rowand Anderson who designed it along 13th-century lines. The fine stained glass windows, depicting Cain, Abel, Jacob and Moses, were created by C.E. Kempe and other Victorian artists.

The Old Parish Church of Govan, following in the steps of its founder St Constantine, has seen involvement with many famous men. Among them were the University Principle and Reformer Andrew Melville, the theological pioneer John MacLeod, and even more famously his clansman George MacLeod (Lord MacLeod of Fuinary) founder of the Iona Community. It was he, who, during the industrial depression of the 1930s, took unemployed men from the shipyards of the Clyde to Iona to rebuild the ruined cathedral which has now become a magnet for pilgrims throughout the world.

In 1994 and 1996 a team of archaeologists from Glasgow University and Channel 4's 'Time Team' were working in the churchyard at Govan when they discovered Christian burials dating back to the 6th, or possibly even the 5th, century. A massive foundation of an early wooden chapel was revealed at the very centre of the enclosure. Remains of craft workshops, also newly uncovered, testified to the skills of the artisans – both monks and laymen – who designed what is recognised as one of the finest collections of monumental sculpture in the British Isles.[13]

Govan became famous as a school of sculpture until, following the Reformation, most of the best examples disappeared or were destroyed as objects of idolatry. In 1762, however, men working in the near circular churchyard dug up a remarkable sarcophagus from beneath the roots of ancient elms.

The centrepiece shows a horseman, riding astride, in pursuit of a stag, and the image is framed by intricate Celtic scroll-work on either side. This stone chest may have held the remains of St Constantine. It was one of three, excavated at the same time, of which the other two have disappeared.

This is an example of the treasures within the 19th-century church which, surrounded by modern building developments, remains significant of the faith of its founder, defiant of advancing time.

St Mirren

Patron Saint of Paisley

St Mirren, who was closely associated with St Constantine, was born of noble parents. As a young boy, his mother entrusted him to the care of Comgall the Great at Bangor in Ulster. He eventually rose to be prior of that famous school of missionaries and somehow he became acquainted with Constantine while the latter

was still King of Cornwall. Interestingly, at
St Mirren, known locally as Har-Llan-Wirran,
there was a church dedicated to
St Constantine, which seems to hint at their
friendship.

Mirren then came to Scotland where he
built a monastery at Paisley only some four
miles from where his friend Constantine had
already become abbot of the church at Govan.

Mirren, like Constantine, travelled widely
in Scotland. Glen Lyon, the longest glen in
Scotland, was a well-known pilgrim trail. One
of the burns that runs into Loch Lyon at
Invermeran, first flows through Glen Meran –
the names of both Inver*meran* and Glen *Meran*
indicating the saint's presence there.

More famously, on the island of
Inchmurrin, which lies at the south end of
Loch Lomond, the saint (from whom the
island's name was evidently taken), built a
chapel. The building stood at the south end of
the thickly wooded island, near the castle of
the Stewart Earls of Lennox. Still visible in the
18th century, it has now sadly disappeared;
doubtless the stones were used for other
purposes as has so frequently occurred.[14]

St Mirren died in Paisley sometime in the
late 6th or early 7th century. The date of his
death was given as 15 September by the
Roman Catholic churchmen who made him
the patron saint of their town. Even today,
crests depicting the saint on the Paisley Coat
of Arms are famously worn by the town's
football club.

A new priory was built on the site of his ancient foundation in the late 12th century. The endowment was created by Walter Stewart, ancestor of the royal house of Stewart, and High Steward to King David I, who granted extensive lands. The priory was dedicated to the Virgin and St Milburga and also, significantly, to St James the Greater of Compostela, patron saint of the Stewarts.[15]

In 1169, Clunian monks from Wenlock in Shropshire, from where the Stewarts came, became the brotherhood of the priory.[16]

The priory became an abbey in 1219. In 1307, however, it was destroyed by the army of the English King Edward II in revenge for the rising of the Scottish hero, William Wallace, who came from Elderslie nearby. Marjorie, daughter of Robert the Bruce (who married a later Walter the Steward), is said to be buried before the altar, as are her son and grandson, Robert II and Robert III.

The nave, rebuilt in the 15th century, remained the parish church. The pilgrim's chapel and the shrine to St Mirren were sited behind the high altar, but so many people flocked to it that in 1499 the abbot, George Shaw, enlarged the south transept to create a larger chapel containing St Mirren's shrine. The decorative sculptured frieze, depicting miracles of the Bible, which surrounds it, although faded in colour, remains a treasured relic today. Incidentally, King James IV received absolution for his connivance in the death of his father from Abbot Shaw in 1491.

So popular did Paisley then become that, by 1500, it was one of the four 'heid' pilgrimages that made up a tour including Melrose, Dundee and Scone, and was regarded as a prime penance.[17]

In 1533, the tower of the church collapsed. The nave, fortunately unscathed, continued as the parish church. The rest of the great building lay in ruins until, in the late 19th and early 20th centuries it was restored by architects (including R. Rowand Anderson and Robert Lorimer) to the state of magnificence in which it stands today. It still remains a magnet, drawing people from all corners of the globe.

ST KESSOG
Saint of Loch Lomond

St Kessog, who was a contemporary of St Fillan and St Serf, was the son of a King of Munster. Trained by St Mochaoi at Nendrum, Kessog sailed from Ireland to begin his missionary work. Making his way from the Clyde estuary up the river Leven, he reached the foot of Loch Lomond and here, on the island of Inchtavanach (which lies close to the west shore near the present village of Luss), he made his home.

The summit of the wooded island is still called Tom na Clog, 'Hill of the Bell'. From here the summons rang out over the water to the people who came by boat to hear him preach and to join with his small community in singing the well loved psalms.

The island proved to be a good centre from which to travel through the wide district of the Lennox, which then stretched from the Clyde to the Forth. Some miles to the east of Loch Lomond, on the Lake of Menteith, St Kessog's friend St Colmac had established a Christian settlement on the island called Inchmocholmoc, now Inchmahome. From there, St Kessog moved to Loch Vennacher, into which runs the Finglas Water from Glen Finglas and Glen Casaif or 'Kessog's Glen'.

Travelling onwards, he went to Callander where a mound near the churchyard called Tom-na Cahessaig again commemorates his name. Ever restless, St Kessog set off again, now following the River Teith and then the Allan Water to Auchterarder where he became the town's patron saint. St Kessog's Day, on 10 March, was for long celebrated by a fair. The ruined chapel of St Kessog, just to the north of the village, was sited near a healing well.

To the west, in the little town of Comrie, in the fertile strath of the Earn, the name of a hill, Tom-na-Chessaig, is interpreted as 'Knoll of St Kessog'.

Once again on the move, St Kessog now ventured farther north. In his time, the mouth of the Beauly Firth could only be crossed by boat. Back and forth he must have sailed, or so testifies the place-names of South Kessock (on the mainland) and North Kessock on the Black Isle. Today, the Kessock Bridge spans the firth so that the road, which by-passes Inverness, now forms the vital link from north to south. Nearby, on Craig Phadrick, the Priséag Well is said to have had the miraculous power to abolish the Evil Eye, thanks to a blessing from St Kessock.

Kessock also travelled along the west coast, preaching the gospel to the people who gathered to hear him in Argyll and further south as far as Kirkcudbright.

Then, suddenly, in 560 his peaceful life was disrupted when the Pictish King Brude MacMailchon attacked the Scots settlers with ferocity, driving most of them back into Argyll. St Kessog, who, as the son of a soldier king, had been trained in archery, seems, with his bow upon his back, to have returned to Lennox to try to save his Christian settlements from destruction.

According to tradition, he was attacked and murdered near Luss (the Gaelic word means 'herbs') near the place of his island home. Here, during the mid-18th century, when soldiers (dubbed the 'Red Coats') were building the military road, they moved part of the pile of stones which are thought to have marked the site of Kessock's first simple chapel, wherein, according to tradition, lies his grave.

St Marnock
of the Sacred Skull

There was once, according to legend, an exceptionally naughty little boy. Brought up in the monastery at Clonmacnois, in Ireland, he was dirty and badly behaved. One day, the building buzzed with excitement – the great missionary Columba was paying a visit. The boy, unnoticed by the monks, crept out and touched the hem of his robe. Columba swung round, grabbed him and held him up to the spectators. 'Let him go!' they cried. 'Why do you touch that unfortunate and naughty boy?' Columba, ignoring them, said to the child, 'My son, open thy mouth, and put out thy tongue.' Too terrified to do otherwise, the boy obeyed whereupon Columba touched and blessed his tongue and to those who watched in amazement, some in disgust, he prophesised that the lad would one day become a teacher of eloquence and power.[18]

Marnock, like Columba, came over to Scotland and apparently sailed up Loch Fyne. Dalvernock, an ancient church-site in Glen Shira, to the east of Inveraray, was believed by the Duke of Argyll to be a corruption of Dalmarnock.[19] Ardmarnock Bay, in Cowal, lies off the east shore of Loch Fyne. In a field called Ardmarnock, the monk is thought to have built a chapel. Here too was the cell where he sought solitude in meditation.

The island of Ardmarnock, some eight miles to the south of Ardmarnock Bay, where he built yet another chapel, lies close to the island of Bute. Christian settlements are known to have been established on Bute by the 7th century. From his island, Marnock is thought to have travelled through the Kyles of Bute. First he landed near Toward, where he built a chapel below Kilmarnock Hill. Heading up the Clyde, he reached Paisley, where he must have found St Mirren. In Glasgow, the place called Dalmarnock bears an association with him, as does the quaintly named Marnock's Portion in Rutherglen.

However, he is mostly famed in Ayrshire, where his original church in Kilmarnock later became the nucleus of the town.

St Marnock went on to travel through the centre of Scotland. Lands held in medieval times by the Abbey of Scone bore his name, as does Dalmarnock, on the Tay (near Dalguise in Perthshire) to the present day. Going ever farther, he is believed to have travelled to Dundee and from there up the east coast to Kincardineshire, before reaching Aberdeen. The ruins of St Marnock's Church at Aboyne still stand on an island in the Dee some three miles from the town.

Aberchirder in Banffshire, once known as Marnock, was where his life's pilgrimage at last came to an end. Again, he built a church by one of the rivers which he so greatly loved. This time it was the Deveron and he lived alongside it, *pulcherrimo Duverne fluvio munita et vallata* ('secured and surrounded by that most beautiful river').[20] Here he died, a very old man, on 1 March 625.

Marnock was buried within his own church where, again, according to the *Aberdeen Breviary*, miracles occurred at his tomb. Before the Reformation, his skull was washed every Sunday and such was the faith of the local people in its efficiency that sick people drank this water believing that they would be cured.[21] The skull was held to be so sacred that oaths were taken before it rather than upon the Bible.

Thus, Columba's forecast came true. The *Breviary* states that such was the majesty and the beauty of Marnock's preaching that *Ita ut tanquam Deum in terries adorarent* – he was adored 'as if he were God on earth'.

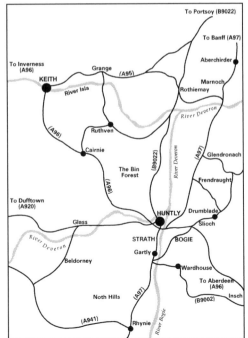

The course of the River Deveron in NE Scotland, beloved by St Marnock

SAINTS OF THE HIGHLANDS & ISLANDS

ST COLUMBA

Pilgrim of the Hebrides

In May 563, a coracle left the coast of Antrim. The boat made of hides, stretched over a wooden frame, traditionally carried 13 men. Their leader, Columba, was of royal blood, descended on his father's side from the famous High King, Niall of the Nine Hostages, and on his mother's from the royal house of Leinster.

Tall and of commanding presence, Columba had reached the peak of his physical power at the age of 42. Nonetheless, he was weighed down by sorrow and by an all-consuming sense of guilt because of the death and mutilation he had caused. At sea, when he had plenty of time to meditate, it must have seemed incredible that this devastation had been caused by a book . . .

The manuscript in question was a codex of the Gospels belonging to his former teacher, Finbar of Moville (himself trained at Candida Casa, at Whithorn) under whom Columba had studied as a young man.

Apparently, Columba had purloined the precious document and made a copy. Furious, Finbar had appealed to the High King Diarmait MacCerball, who had ordered Columba to return the facsimile he had made.

Columba was already at enmity with King Diarmait and so had responded by calling out the Clan Niall against him. The two sides had fallen upon each other at Cooldrevny, near Sligo. Columba had been victorious but many on both sides had been slain. King Diarmait then inflicted his revenge by calling a congress of Irish churchmen who excommunicated Columba.

The sentence was repealed, but Columba, tortured by his own conscience, had accepted the advice of his confessor, Molaise of Devenish, to exile himself from Ireland and win souls for Christ in other lands.

So it was that he set sail with great sadness, leaving all that was dear to him. Uppermost in his thoughts was the monastery which he himself had founded in Derry, land of his birth.

> *The reason why I love Derry is*
> *For its quietness, for its purity,*
> *Crowded full of Heaven's angels*
> *Is every leaf of the oaks of Derry.*
> *My Derry, my little oak-grove,*
> *My dwelling, and my little cell.*
> *Oh eternal God in Heaven above!*
> *Woe be to him who violates it.*

Thus runs the translation of the Latin words attributed to a man who condemned himself to exile from the homeland of his heart.

> *I have loved Erin's land of cascades,*
> *All but its government.*

And as Ireland faded from view he wrote:

> *My vision o'er the brine I stretch*
> *From the ample oaken planks:*
> *Large is the tear of my soft grey eye*
> *When I look back upon Erin.*

The boat followed a course which, in all probability, led it to Rathlin Isle, then across to Islay, then north past Jura where the men aboard her could hear the dreaded thunder of the whirlpool of Corryvrecken between Jura and Scarba. Reputedly, Columba landed on Colonsay, but on climbing a hill on Oronsay (the island connected to Colonsay by a tidal strand) and seeing that the smudge of Ireland on the horizon was still visible, he knew that he must not stay. His punishment was incomplete. He had to go on.

The sea became rough, the sky darkened with scudding cloud. No longer could he plot his position by sun and stars. The men with him cowered into the bottom of the boat but Columba relished the danger as the storm drove the devils from his mind. Lost, they expected to die, as in darkness their frail craft crashed against rocks. But Columba cried aloud to God and 'swelling waves also, that once in a great storm rose like mountains, quickly subsided at his prayer, and were stilled. And his ship, in which he himself chanced to be sailing, was at that time, when the calm fell, carried to the desired haven.'[1]

He had, in fact, reached Iona lying off the south-west tip of Mull. The boat came ashore in the inlet on the south shore which is known as Port na Curaich to this day. Traversing the island to the north, he climbed Calva Dun, at 101 metres the highest point, and to his great relief saw the ocean before him stretching unbroken to the sky. He had found his refuge. Little did he or his companions know, as they scrambled stiff legged on to the shingle, that they were the first in a line of many pilgrims that future centuries would bring.

Most authorities now agree that Iona was not the first place where St Columba set foot in Argyll. Apparently, he had been before (probably in the previous year) to treat with Conall, King of the Scots of Dal Riata. Conall, it seems, had sent a message begging for assistance in his struggle to defend Argyll – at that time colonised by Scots from Northern Ireland for some 60 years – against aggressive Picts.

Columba is claimed to have come ashore at Southend, on the south coast of Kintyre. Standing upon the knoll above the now ruined medieval church, which bears his name, he would have preached to the local

St Columba's Footprints

The knoll from where Columba is said to have preached. The footprints are, in fact, two right feet, between which the figures 564 have been rudely incised. It is known that although the southern one may be 1,000 years old, the other was the work of a local stonemason no earlier than 1856!

people gathered on the shore below. From Southend he made his way, either on foot or more probably by sea (round the Mull of Kintyre), to the mouth of the River Add, near Crinan. This region was under the rule of Conall, whose fort was sited on top of the hill of Dunadd. After some discussion, Conall, subservient to his Pictish overlord, reputedly 'granted' Iona to Columba as a place to settle with his monks.

Winter was now approaching. A sea passage to the island of Iona would have been excessively dangerous in this season of storms and Columba is said to have spent the winter in a cave (still called 'St Columba's Cave') at the head of Loch Caolisport – the sea loch running north-west from the sound of Jura into Knapdale in Argyll. A roughly hewn platform of rock within the cave supports a simple stone altar. A small cross is carved above. A deep circular basin by the entrance has been scooped out of the rock, suggestive of a baptismal font. In another cave behind, where the ground has been hollowed out like an animal's lair, the monks are believed to have slept.[2]

Now reconcilled to King Diarmait and his council, Columba returned to Ireland to confer with them on policies concerning the protection of the colony of Scots settlers in Dal Riata in Argyll. Columba, the evangelist, was also an ambassador of the Irish king.

St Columba returned from Ireland to Iona in the following year to begin what Adomnan (later the Abbot of Iona, his first biographer) calls 'his pilgrimage to Britain'. It lasted for 34 years until the time of Columba's death in 597.

From Iona, he journeyed far and wide. Most famously, he travelled to Inverness to treat with the Pictish King Brude. On this journey his most direct route by boat would have been round the Ross of Mull, into the Firth of Lorn and from there to the head of Loch Linnhe. The River Lochy may have been partly navigable, but as the tall figure of the saint strode ahead, his companions resorted to porterage, carrying the coracle of wood bound with tarred hides to Loch Lochy along the riverbank. Adomnan uses the Latin phrase *fatigatio iteneris* to describe this journey, which is translated as 'the labour of a steep path'.

Having spent one night by a burn which ran into the Lochy (probably on the north shore), the party then crossed the watershed above Loch Oich and sailed on down Loch

Ness. Adomnan relates the miraculous story of Columba's crossing of the River Ness. 'When he reached its bank, he saw a poor fellow being buried by other inhabitants [who] said that, while swimming not long before, he had been seized and most savagely bitten by a water beast . . . When the blessed man heard this, he ordered, not withstanding, that one of his companions should swim out and bring back to him, by sailing, a boat that stood on the opposite bank . . . Lugne Mocumin obeyed without delay, and putting off his clothes, excepting his tunic, plunged into the water. But the monster, whose appetite had earlier been not so much sated but whetted for prey, lurked in the depth of the river. Feeling the water above disturbed by Lugne's swimming, it suddenly swam up to the surface, and with a gaping mouth and with great roaring rushed towards the man swimming in the middle of the stream. While all that were there, barbarians and even the brothers, were struck down with extreme terror, the blessed man, who was watching, raised his holy hand and drew the saving sign of the cross in the empty air; and then, invoking the name of God, he commanded the savage beast, and said: 'You will go no further. Do not touch the man; turn back speedily.' Then hearing this command of the saint, the beast, as if pulled back with ropes, fled terrified in swift retreat . . .

Then, seeing that the beast had withdrawn and that their fellow soldier

Lugne had returned to them unharmed and safe, in the boat, the brothers with great amazement glorified God in the blessed man. And also the pagan barbarians who were there at the time, impelled by the magnitude of this miracle that they themselves had seen, magnified the God of the Christians.' Thus, the first sighting of the Loch Ness Monster is graphically described.

Columba, on reaching Brude's fortress, near Inverness, found himself confronted by the locked gates of the surrounding wooden palisade. 'First imprinting the sign of the Lord's cross upon the doors, he knocked, and laid his hand upon them. And immediately the doors were forcibly drawn back, and the doors opened of themselves with all speed. As soon as they were open the saint entered with his associates.

Learning this, the king with his council was much alarmed, and left the house, and went to meet the blessed man with reverence; and addressed him very pleasantly with words of peace. And from that day onwards, throughout the rest of his life, that ruler greatly honoured the holy and venerable man, as was fitting, with high esteem.'

Miraculously, Columba restored a dead boy to life and healed the magician Broichan, foster-father of King Brude, who had swallowed parts of a goblet which shattered as he was drinking. He then further astounded the Picts by sailing up Loch Ness in a fierce storm contrary to the wind.

An expert in navigation, he visited many of the islands which lie off the west coast. Adomnan tells us that he was 'for some days on the island of Sci' [Skye] where a wild boar fell dead 'slain by the power of his terrible word'. He is said to have founded a now vanished monastery near Monkstead, north of Uig Bay. On the east coast, on the island of Eilean Columkille, in the inner bay of Portree (mentioned by Adomnan) traces of an ancient chapel and graves can still be found.[3]

Adomnan states that Columba built a chapel on the island of Trodday off the north-west point of Skye. The historian and well-known naturalist, Martin Martin, himself a Skye man and factor for the MacLeods of Dunvegan, claims that the saint founded another on the even more remote island of Fladda-Chuain 'Fladda of the ocean' in the Minch.

Traditionally, Columba built a cell on Eilean-an-Tigh 'Island of the House' largest of the Shiant islands which lie off the east coast of Lewis still farther to the north.

In Lewis, on the Eye Peninsula, stands the Old Kirk of Eye. Later rebuilt, the original foundations are attributed to St Columba's time. The cemetery on the island of Eilean Chaluim Cille, at the mouth of Loch Erisort, surrounds St Columba's Church. The stretch of water called Loch Colunkille is farther north.

St Columba is said to have built a chapel on Bernera. A ruin half buried in sand on

Beehive cells on Eilach a Naoimh, one of the Garvellach Islands which was St Columba's favourite retreat

North Uist is called Kilchalumkill. Teampull Cholumcille is near Ballivanich in Benbecula, and a chapel at Howmore, in South Uist, is dedicated to the saint. Intrepid voyager as he was, he is credited with having sailed even as far as St Kilda, where a chapel, long since ruined, bears his name.

On Tiree, the granary of the islands, Columba built a monastery near Soroby. The original building has vanished although a chapel of later date stands on what is probably the same site. Another chapel, beside the 14th-century parish church of Kirkapol above Gott Bay (dedicated to St Columba) may also have been founded in his day.[4]

Adomnan writes of Columba in Mull where the parish of Kilcolmkill perpetuates his memory. Also Sailean Dubh Chaluim Chille near Torosay on the Sound of Mull, means 'Dark Salen of St Columba'.

Suidheachan Chaluimchille, or 'St Columba's seat', a mile from Bunessan, stands within an ancient stone circle and may signify the triumph of Christianity over the pagan gods.

The Garvellachs – Isles of the Sea – lie between Mull and Scarba in the Firth of Lorn and legend has it that Eileach an Naoimh, 'Rock of the Saints', was St Columba's favourite place of retreat. Close to a ruined chapel are the monk's beehive cells. A natural rock pulpit stands beside the shore. The saint must have preached to the brethren, his voice ringing out on the wind, above the surge of the sea.

The foundations of a monastery lie on level ground by the shore. Above, on the top of a small hill, is the grave said to be that of the Irish princess Eithne, Columba's mother. Perhaps this is why this remote sea-girt island became a spiritual haven for this restless dedicated man.

Linocut of St Columba
by Dom Ninian Sloane
(Pluscarden Abbey)

Columba made many visits to the mainland. He is known to have gone to Ardnamurchan at least three times. Adomnan describes him performing miracles both in Lochaber and in Glenurchat, where he cleansed a polluted well.

Most famously, as leader of Gaelic
monasticism in the west of Scotland,
Columba travelled to meet St Kentigern,
Bishop of Glasgow and head of the Brito-
Pictish Church of the centre and east of
Scotland. The two holy men met and
embraced at the Molendinar burn. They spent
days together in conversation until their
peace was disturbed when some of
Columba's followers attacked Kentigern's
shepherds and killed the fattest of the sheep.
The crime was avenged by a miracle – the
thieves were turned to stone. However,
thanks to Kentigern's prayers, the men were
restored to life. Both saints parted as brothers
in Christ but were never to meet again.[5]

Nonetheless, it is the islands which hold
most memory of St Columba, he who sailed
so fearlessly into the storms. The little ruined
chapels remain to honour his name. He died
on Iona on 9 June 597, his pilgrimages at a
final end . . .

Following his death, the Celtic and Pictish
missionaries, later to be canonised, continued
the evangelism with which his life had been
inspired. Their stories, though embellished by
legend, nonetheless prove them to be the
pilgrims who, in the savage times of early
recorded history, carried the torch of
Christianity to remote corners of Scotland and
the Isles.

St Donnan
the Red-haired Martyr

Donnan was an Irish Pict who came over to Scotland from his native land to spread the word of God. He first went to Candida Casa, in Galloway, where he gathered a band of 52 disciples whom he trained and sent forth to preach. Afterwards, having crossed the Bay of Luce to the Mull of Galloway, he founded several churches there before sailing to the Isle of Man.

Once back in Scotland, he spent some time preaching in Ayrshire where traces of the primitive chapels which he built can still be found. In Arran, near Kildonan Castle, the ruins of Kildonan Chapel – 27 feet long and 10 feet wide – still stand looking over the sea.

Leaving Arran, Donnan headed for Kintyre where the ruins of the church and churchyard, which he is thought to have built, stand about five miles north of Campbeltown near Ballochgair farm. It is lovely peaceful place which looks across to Arran, but Donnan's restless spirit would not let him remain.

With his band of followers, he sailed to Iona. St Columba greeted him as a fellow Christian and Donnan, recognising the intensity of his faith, asked him to be his *ammchara*, the Gaelic word for 'soul-mate'. Expecting immediate acceptance, he was shocked and bitterly disappointed when

Columba refused his request telling him 'I shall not be soul-friend to a company of red martyrdom, for thou shalt come to red martyrdom, and thy people with thee.'[6]

Donnan, upon hearing this, left Iona both mortified and apprehensive of what a known visionary had foreseen. Brave as he was, he must by now have known that Norse raiders, based in Orkney, were raiding the north of Scotland leaving death and destruction in their wake.

Nonetheless, Donnan sailed on, back to the mainland of Scotland where, once again, helped by his band of companions, he continued to build chapels – Kildonan, at Munerigie, at the foot of Loch Garry, is known to have been the site of one.

Again he moved on, this time to Sutherland where at Kildonan, on the Helmsdale, he founded 'a large and spacious establishment which might serve many of the purposes which Candida Casa in the far south had fulfilled'.[7] His cell was near the Ulligh where fragments of the rock, from which he preached to the people on the other side when the river was too high to cross, remain on the bank. Ulligh is the old Gaelic name of the Helmsdale river, and the Strath of Kildonan was also known as the the Strath of Ulligh.

Donnan's disciples travelled far and wide from Helmsdale preaching the word of God. They returned bringing news of the ever increasing terror of the Viking raids. Donnan, mindful of Columba's warning, moved to Little Loch Broom in Ross-shire where the ruins of Cladh Chill Donnain and the bay called Corran Chill Donnain bear testimony to his name. Travelling on, he is believed to have built a chapel within a traditional grave-yard called Seipeil Donnain at Courthill, near the entrance to Loch Carron, and another on Eilean Donan where the castle now stands.[8]

Still searching for a safe place to settle, he crossed to Skye, where Kildonan, in the parish of Snizort, is thought to have been his home for a brief time. Moving on again, he founded a chapel called Kildonan, in the remote island of Little Bernera, off the west coast of Lewis. Then, in South Uist, in the parish of Kilpeter, he built yet another Kildonan Church on the machair fringing the Atlantic.

Driven by his conviction that somewhere his chosen haven was yet to be found, he voyaged on yet again, together with his faithful following, eastwards to the Small Isles off the north coast of Ardnamurchan. Approaching, they saw the island of Eigg so clearly recognisable by its ragged Scuir – the block of pitchstone and lava founded on an old river-bed – stark as a shark's fin against the sky.

Donnan came ashore on the east end of the island where he built a chapel and a dormitory to house his brethren. He believed he could live here in safety for the people were of his own Pictish race. In addition, the light soil of the land near the shore would grow enough grain for them to survive. Alas he was mistaken. Here there was a new enemy, a woman more deadly than any man.

She seems to have been a princess, or a chieftainess, who dominated the nearby mainland of Arisaig. Furious at what she considered to be an annexation of grazing pasture for her cattle, she sent word to the people of Eigg to destroy the settlers, threatening them with death themselves should her orders be disobeyed.

Waiting then for the heads of her victims to be sent to her in proof of their deaths, she realised eventually that the brave people on the island, who had grown to love the Christian men, were risking their own lives in defying her commands. Furious, she sent a messenger to find the Norsemen who were rumoured to have sailed from the north of Scotland to the Western Isles. They needed no encouragement. The long-boats headed for Eigg . . .

On the morning of Sunday, 17 April 612, the raiders came ashore. It is said to have been a day so still that the voices of the brethren singing carried down from the church. Clutching their deadly double-edged axes, which could strike a man's head off at a blow, the Norsemen descended on the little building and crashed open the door.

Donnan, turning from the altar to face them, asked only that he and his brethren might have time to celebrate their communion before meeting their deaths. The Norsemen, stunned at their courage, agreed. The service ended and Donnan led his men to the refectory so 'that the place where God had been worshipped in spiritual joy might not be polluted with their blood, and that they should rather die in the room where they had gratified their bodily appetites'.

Within minutes they smelt burning as the pirates thrust flaming torches into the thatched roof. The wood and wattle building caught fire almost immediately. Then, with the men trapped within, it burnt quickly to the ground.

Thus, on a peaceful Sunday morning, Donnan, later to be canonised as a saint, fulfilled the prophesy of Columba, when, together with his followers (believed to be 52 in all), he died the death of a martyr for the faith he so devotedly upheld.

The islands of Eigg and Rhum. It was on Eigg, which lies to the west, that St Donnan was murdered by Norsemen on the orders of a Pictish princess

St Moluag

and the Green Isle of Lismore

S t Columba was not without jealousy, if legend be true. The story runs that he and St Moluag were rivals in establishing a religious centre on Lismore, the island which lies in Loch Linnhe, just off the Appin shore.

The legend tells of how St Moluag, approaching the island, saw Columba's birlinn overtaking his own. Placing his hand on the gunwhale, he severed his little finger with an axe and threw the finger on to the shore, shouting in Gaelic, 'My flesh and blood have first possession of the island, and I bless it in the name of the Lord.'

Columba, furious at being outdone, cursed the rocks, saying they would grow edge-uppermost.

'They will hurt no one to walk on them,' retorted Moluag.

'May you have the alder for your fuel!' stormed Columba.

'Yet it will burn like tinder.' Moluag yelled back in triumph.

True enough, today the strata on the eastern side of the island appear to be vertically upturned but, being composed of limestone, are easy on the feet. Also alder, which can smoke abominably, burns well on Lismore.

The animosity between these holy men, if

it existed, seems to have been rooted in race. St Columba was a Scot of royal ancestry, St Moluag, although well born, was nonetheless a Pict.

Adomnan describes Columba as aesthetic, tall and thin to the point where his ribs showed through his cassock. Moluag was probably small, stocky, and red-haired, in common with most of his people.

Moluag, like Columba, was born in Ireland and trained for the priesthood under St Comgall at Bangor. He came to Scotland and for a time served under St Baithene, Columba's cousin, in the monastery founded by the latter at Soroby in Tiree.

St Moluag came ashore at Port Moluag on the north-east point of Lismore. He is said to be buried there within the first chapel, now long vanished, which he built. More famously, he founded a church farther inland on the site of the Parish Church of today.

Lismore Parish Church, built partly on the site of the Cathedral of St Moluag, centre of the diocese of Argyll c.1183

Lismore, in the 11th century, was part of the enormous diocese of Dunkeld. Administration over such a widespread area, linked only by waterways and tracks across the hills, proved to be so impossible that the diocese of Argyll was formed *c*.1183. The chapel built by St Moluag, enlarged to include a choir, became a cathedral in the early 14th century.[9]

A broken cross, called *Clach na h'eala*, 'stone of the swan', stands near the church. Close by the outlines of ancient walls are traditionally those of 'a sanctuary where malefactors of every description fled for refuge, during the darkness of past ages . . . And it is said that the malefactor fleeing to the sanctuary was safe, when once he laid his hand on the horn of the altar, *Clach na h'eala*, and after remaining a year and a day within the walls, he came out absolved of his crimes.'[10]

The now ruined Achadun Castle stands above steep cliffs at the western end of Lismore high above the sea. Built during the 13th century, it was protected by a strong curtain wall.

Achadun Bay is a good anchorage into which chiefs of the Highlands and the Isles, churchmen and many pilgrims sailed in to confer with the bishops and to pray for their soul's salvation within the cathedral walls.

In 1462, George Lauder, Bishop of Argyll, fled from his castle to seek refuge within the church as the galleys of MacDonalds from

Islay were seen approaching from the sea. Donald Balloch, leader of the raiders, had a score to settle with Lauder, who had put his seal to an order for the arrest of the Earl of Douglas with whom Balloch was in league. Lauder escaped unscathed within the cathedral's stone walls, but the Islesmen torched the thatched roofs of the wood and wattle huts of the local people and stole or killed the animals and crops on which their lives depended.

Despite the destruction of the raiders, Lismore remained a place of pilgrimage for people from near and far. The island, lying as it does in Loch Linnhe, between the Lynn of Morvern and the Linn of Lorn, was on the main route for travellers following the age-old route which St Columba took through Loch Lochy and Loch Ness.

Following the Reformation, the Cathedral became the Parish Church.

Pilgrimages were forbidden by the Presbyterian creed, but nonetheless people were drawn to this quiet and beautiful place even as they are today.

Lismore can be reached by car ferry from Oban or by the launch which takes foot passengers to and from Port Appin across the Lynn of Lorn.

St Moluag's Chair, Lismore

St Maelrubha
of the Fiery Hair

Another red-haired saint was Maelrubha, born in Londonderry on 3 January 642. On his father's side, he was descended from the famous Ard Irish Ardrigh, or high king, Niall of the Nine Hostages. St Columba's father, Phelim MacFergus, was the great-grandson of the king. Thus, Maelrubha was a distant cousin of Columba.[11] On his mother's side, Maelrubha was connected to St Comgall of Bangor, Ulster, who was a Pict. Perhaps it was through her that he inherited his flaming red hair, symbolic of the energy which surged within his frame.

Maelrubha was educated in the Missionary Institute founded by Comgall at Bangor. In 671, when he was 29, he set forth on an evangelical mission to Scotland. With him went a band of disciples. Searching for the right place to build a monastic settlement, they first sailed up the long sea inlet of Loch Fyne to land at Strathlachlan on the west coast of Cowal.

Here he founded a church named 'Kilmorie', probably on the site of the now ruined late 16th-century church which stands below the road near Castle Lachlan. The chiefs of Clan Lachlan and their families lie buried within the churchyard.[12]

Moving south to Kintyre, Maelrubha is

The Chapel of Kilmory Knap and the MacMillan
Cross of the Loch Sween (Suibhne) School,
which dates from the late 15th century

said to have built a now vanished church in
Glen Barr where local places bear his name.
On Islay, in the parish of Kilarrow, he built a
church at Bridgend at the head of Lochindaal
and today you can see ancient stones in the
burial ground.

Returning to the mainland, he is believed
to have founded what was probably a
wooden church on the site of the 13th-century
chapel at Kilmory Knap, on the south shore of
Loch Suibhne.

Again heading north, he sailed up
through the Sound of Jura to land on the
north shore of Loch Craignish. Here he
founded a Christian settlement on the site of
Kilmarie Parish Church.[13]

Within the walls of the now roofless 13th-
century building stand two Early Christian

slabs of the local quartzitic gneiss which are carved with the emblems of a Latin Cross. They must have been objects of veneration for the medieval church, when it was built, was dedicated to St Maelrubha of Applecross as he had by then become.

Sailing round the headland of Craignish, Maelrubha found his way to Loch Melfort. He is claimed to have founded a chapel at Kilmelfort, at the head of Loch Melfort. Heading north over land, he followed the road which runs from Kilmore at the head of Loch Feochan, an inlet from the Firth of Lorn, to the village of Connel on Loch Etive. He built a chapel at Kilmarrow (now Kilvarie) and *Eialean-an-t-Sagairt*, the priest's island, on the Black Loch, just west of Connel, is said to have been the site of Maelrubha's cell.

Nearby at Dunstaffnage Castle, the now ruined chapel is called 'Kilmorrie'. The legend runs that Malrubha set off from here, heading east beyond the mountains of Drumalban, which marked, at that time, the western boundaries of land held by the Picts. From the head of Glen Etive, with his men probably carrying his coracle, his most likely route was by the old track to Black Corries, then across the Moor of Rannoch to Loch Rannoch. From the foot of Loch Tummel they would have headed over the moor below Schiehallion down to Kenmore at the foot of Loch Tay and from there continued over the watershed and down to Loch Freuchie, beyond which lies Amulree. The fact that

'Amulree' means 'the ford of Maelrubha' may
indicate that it became a centre for his
missionary journeys for some time.

Maelrubha, like his fellow Pict, Donnan,
could never rest. His travels along the east
coast are remembered in a variety of ways. A
priory in the fishing village of Crail on the
Firth of Forth, originally dedicated to 'Sanct
Maruiff' later became 'St Rufus' in token of
the colour of his hair. A fair used to be held
on St Maelrubha's Day, 27 August, in Pitlessie
in Fife. Two churches in Forfar are said to be
built on sites of the small chapels which he
built, most probably of wood and turf.

From Amulree, he retraced his steps west,
seeking his familiar territory of mountains
girt by the sea. Having sailed round
Ardnamurchan, Maelrubha came ashore at
Arisaig Bay. The now ruined Pre-Reformation
Church of Kilmaroy (sometimes called Cill
Marui) was built, according to tradition,
where once Maelrubha lived. Here in this
peaceful spot above a safe anchorage he
might have been satisfied, yet ever onwards
he went, still searching for the place which he
meant to make his own. His eyes were on the
land as his men rowed and sailed the coracle
through the Sound of Sleat to Loch Alsh.
Then, rounding the east end of Skye, they
were into the Inner Sound.

Raasay lay to the west, beneath the
towering mountains of Skye. To the east, on
the mainland, they spied what looked to be a
safe landing-place at the mouth of a green

strath. Stepping ashore from the coracle, Maelrubha knew instinctively that at last he had found his home.

Applecross, first known as 'Apurcrossan', lies at the head of its sheltered bay. High mountains shield it on the landward side. Maelrubha found it a haven. He was now among his own people, the Picts. In 673, he founded his sanctuary, or *muinntir*, which is said to have stretched around his church for a radius of six miles in all directions, the boundary being marked out by stones inscribed with the Christian cross, of which only part of one remains.

Maelrubha, so long without roots, remained at Applecross for 49 years, so it is little wonder that a number of places are named after him. *Tober-ma-Rui* – the well of Maelrubha – was a venue for pilgrims who believed the water had healing powers. A bell, which he hung on a tree near the church, is said to have rung on Sundays, without the aid of human hand, summoning local people to worship. Removed eventually to the church called *Cill-Chriosd* which replaced Maelrubha's original foundation, it remained silent and the tree on which it was hanging soon died.

From Applecross, Maelrubha often crossed the Inner Sound to Skye. The chapel which he is said to have built on the north side of Loch Eishort was called Kilmoree. Another chapel situated at the head of Loch Eynort was called Kilmalrui. St Maelrubha's

Church at Borline, built on the site of his earlier foundation, contained an elaborately carved font which is now in the National Museum of Antiquities in Edinburgh. Carvings depict the Crucifixion, St Michael with his sword, the Virgin and Child, and a bishop wearing a mitre which must be St Maelrubha.

In the north of Skye, he built another church near Quiraing called Kilmaroy.

From Skye – probably from Uig from where the modern-day ferry sails – Maelrubha crossed the Little Minch to Harris. The ruin of a small chapel on the south side of the peninsula of Toe Head, on the south shore of Loch Seaforth is called 'Malrube'. However, Martin Martin, a Skye man who, as well as being factor for the MacLeods of Dunvegan in the late 1600s, was also a historian, refers to it as 'St Rufus' – another example of how the red-headed evangelist was known by two names.

St Rufus crops up again in the Croullin Islands, which lie between Raasay and Applecross in the Inner Sound. The smallest and most northerly Eilean Beg – known as 'St Rufus Isle' – contains the foundations of a church about 30 feet in length.

Heading back towards the mainland, Maelrubha sailed up Loch Carron to create a settlement at Clachan Mulruy (Village of Mulrubha). The burn called Alt-an-Sagairt – 'the Priest's Stream' – is just beyond the site of his church. From here, intrepid as ever, this

Pictish priest, later to be sanctified for his zeal, pursued his way up the Carron and over the watershed into Strath Bran. Continuing from there, still heading east to Garve and then south–east to Strathpeffer, he reached Dingwall and the Cromarty Firth.

Further south, in the Black Isle, he established a church at Urquart. Then, crossing via the Chanonry Ferry, he arrived at Forres where he is said to have built a church in nearby Rafford. Moving east again, along the south shore of the Moray Firth, he found his way to Keith where, finally, he is credited with having established a small Christian community on the coast in what is now the fishing village of Portsoy.

Eventually, after a period of many years, he retired, perhaps with thankfulness, to his sanctuary of Applecross. Aware by now that the strength of his youth was failing, he travelled less, sending his disciples to preach the Gospel in his place. Yet despite physical frailty he became so greatly venerated that his name was bestowed on the most beautiful stretch of water in the North-West Highlands: Loch Maree.

Within the loch are 27 islands, mostly wooded, which in summer lie green against the water which, when still, reflects the rock-bound heights of Ben Slioch. On one, significantly named 'Eilean Marui', are the remains of a chapel within a burial ground. Close by, on the shore of the loch, is Maelrubha's Well. People affected by mental illness came, or were brought from afar, convinced that the water cured insanity.

Maelrubha was now approaching 80, a great age for his time. His bones most likely ached with rheumatism and his once imposing stature must have been bent. Nevertheless, his spirit drove him to set off on yet another expedition which would have daunted many younger men.

Sailing up Loch Broom, or following the shore on foot, he was, for some reason, forced to turn back. According to an old legend, this was because he was confronted by Norsemen, but historians tell us that that their raiding in this area had not yet begun. Therefore, it seems more probable that physical exhaustion was the cause. Returning to Loch Torridon, he headed east, stopping firstly at Suidhe ma Rui, near Kinlochewe, and then at a place of the same name at the east end of Loch Rosque. Plagued by increasing infirmity, he now preached sitting upon stones – Suidhe ma Rui means 'Maelrubha's seat'.

From Achnasheen, he headed to Garve and then up Strath Oykel to Loch Shin where, on the island of Innes-ma-Rui, he built the first recorded church in the parish of Lairg. St Mourie's Fair – for long held yearly in the little town – commemorated the saint's influence.

In Sutherland, at Durness, near to the church supposedly founded by St Maelrubha, a hollow rock called Clach na Sagairt Ruaidh means 'the stone of the red priest'.

St Maelrubha died in his 80s in 722. The grave, claimed to be his, can be seen in Applecross, the place of his heart's desire. However, Dr G.A. Frank Knight disputes this, claiming that Clach ma Rui does not mean 'Maelrubha's grave' but the 'Cemetery of Maelrubha' or, in other words, the place where his followers were buried.

Even the legendary death of St Maelrubha is shrouded in mystery and appears to have become confused with that of the 'Red Priest', another Pictish evangelist who also had flaming red hair.

Certainly a 'Red Priest', whatever his identity, was connected with Strathnaver. At Skaill, some ten miles from the foot of Loch Naver, there is a chambered cairn. A man could have sheltered here, safe from prowling wolves. Close by is 'Cnocan an t Sagairt Rhuaidh' the 'Hill of the Red Priest'.

Below lies a wood where Maelrubha, or his counterpart, the 'Red Priest,' was preaching to the local people when 'Danish pirates', who had landed at the mouth of the river, crept up amongst the trees.

They slaughtered him without mercy before, according to tradition, dragging his butchered body into the bushes of the copse. Here his disciples found him and buried him near where he was killed.

At Skail, beside the river (in the far corner of the field directly opposite the car park) stands an early Christian monument – a round-topped shaft inscribed with a Greek

Cross. Is this the place where St Maelrubha, that restless and dauntless pilgrim of Christ was at last laid to rest? Or is it the grave of the priest with the red hair with whom he has become confused?

Dr Kevin O'Reilly, in his excellent guide book *What to See in Strathnaver* says that the Viking raids in Sutherland didn't begin until 795. Therefore the 'Red Priest,' whom they slew and whose stone stands at Skaill by the River Naver, cannot have been St Maelrubha.

What is known is that Maelrubha, like Columba, had always longed for Ireland, the birthplace from which he had sailed so many years before. His epitaph in the *Felire of Oengus* describes his love for his homeland and for the mother whom he left as a young man never to see again.

> *In Alba, in purity,*
> *After abandoning all happiness,*
> *Hath gone from us to his mother,*
> *Our brother Maelrubha.*

Applecross, the sanctuary of Maelrubha

St Cathan

S t Cathan, or Cathanan, as his name is sometimes spelt, was an Irish Pict, related both to St Moluag and St Comgall. Following St Comgall's founding of his famous missionary school at Bangor, in 558, Cathan there received the strict training of a monk.

Leaving Ireland, he sailed across to Scotland and established his own monastery in Bute. It stood on the south-east end of the island overlooking Kilchattan Bay, near to the church which was later to be founded by Cathan's nephew, St Blane.

From a hill above the bay he could look out to the Cumbraes and beyond to the mainland across Kilbrannon Sound. To the south, the mountains of Arran stood stark against the sky and to the west, on clear days, he could see across the Sound of Bute to Kintyre.

His retreat was remote and beautiful, but Cathan, like so many of his contemporaries, was restless with missionary zeal. He built chapels in Islay and Jura before moving to Colonsay where, on the west side of the island, the ruins of the old church of Kilchattan stand within a churchyard. Close by was the well, called *Tobar Chattan*, where the water was thought to be blessed by the holy man.

The little island of Gigha, 'God's Isle', lies

close to the west coast of Kintyre. Here, St Cathan built a chapel near the head of Ardminish Bay, just north of Achamore House. Again, it stood beside a holy well, some few metres south of the burial ground.

Later, in the 13th century, the old parish churches of Gigha and its neighbouring island, Cara, were built on the sites of St Cathan's chapels. Now only part of the walls remain, but the font, mentioned by Martin Martin in 1695 when the church was still in use, has been moved to the current parish church, which stands on another site.

Again travelling north, Cathan reached the island of Luing. His original chapel, probably built of wood and turf, near Toberonoch was replaced by a stone building in the 12th century. Rough carvings on the outside stones of the three remaining walls show Highland galleys and crosses, one being a Greek cross of pre-Reformation date.

The church remained in use until 1735. The parish of Kilchattan – comprising the islands of Luing, Shuna and Torsa, together with some smaller islands – was united with Kilbrandon at a now forgotten date.

From Luing, Cathan sailed up Loch Etive where, on the sun-blessed south-facing north shore, he is believed to have found the almost perfect spot for one of his simple chapels.

Some six centuries later, in 1193, a priory was founded on this same site by Duncan MacDougall, Lord of Lorn. It was gifted to the Valliscaullian order (founded originally in

France by Eudes III, Duke of Burgundy).

The name 'Val des Choux' has for centuries been taken to mean 'Valley of the Cabbages'. The 'Brethren of the Cabbage-Valley' was formally confirmed by Pope Innocent III on 12 February 1265.[14]

Recent research, however, has revealed that the original name was probably 'Valley of the Owls'. The area is heavily wooded and therefore much more conducive to the habitation of owls rather than the cultivation of cabbages. *Chouette* is French for owl; 'chou', being a common shortening of the word.

This throws a different light on the emblems on the walls at Ardchattan which have been thought to be cabbages for hundreds of years. Cabbage stalks resemble carrots, which are known to be fertility symbols of medieval times. Also the carvings, now much worn by weather, do bear a resemblance to the heads of the pagan god, the Green Man, in Rosslyn Chapel and other medieval churches. From this it seems reasonable to assume that fertility symbols, not cabbages, are depicted on the priory walls.

Val des Choux in Burgundy was a staging-post for pilgrims travelling from central and eastern Europe to Santiago de Compostela, in north-west Spain. Believed to hold the tomb of St James the Great, Santiago de Compostela was the great goal of all pilgrims from far and wide.

Ardchattan Priory, founded by Duncan
MacDougall, Lord of Lorn, c.1230

Situated in the remote West Highlands of
Scotland, on the inlet where Loch Etive meets
the sea, Ardchattan was convenient to the
network of ferries which linked the tracks
across the hills. The monks gave shelter and
succour to travellers who came in mostly by
boat, or from the landward side down Gleann
Salach, before continuing on their way.

St Cathan himself is supposed to have
gone to Ardnamurchan where 'Clach Chatain'
means burying place of Chattan, although,
because he is known to have loved it, his own
foundation at Kilchattan in Bute may be his
final resting place.

TRIUMPHANT BLANE
of the Britons

St Blane of Kingarth, or St Blaan, as he is sometimes called, was a nephew of St Cathan. When the latter sailed from Ireland to Bute, he came with his sister, Ertha, or Bertha, who gave birth to the son of an unknown father. Cathan, on discovering this, put both mother and child in a boat without oars and set them afloat. The coracle carried them across the Irish Sea to Bethorne, in Northern Ireland, where St Comgall and St Kenneth, both contemporaries of St Columba, gave them a safe home.

Blane was trained, first by Comgall, and later by Kenneth, either in his monastery at Achabo, or when he was in Fife. The story goes that the boy, aged only seven, then went back to Kilchattan Bay in Bute to become reconciled to his uncle whom he eventually succeeded as Bishop of Kingarth.

On the south-east of the island, just north of Garrochy Head, at Kilblane in Kingarth, he built a monastery. Traces of what seem to have been a circular building may indicate the site, although parts of it appear to have been incorporated during the 12th century into a Norman church. St Blane's Well, nearby, is three feet wide and deep, the sides being built up with stones. *Suidhe Bhlain* means 'Blane's seat', while a hollow in one of the stones is claimed to be an imprint of his foot. More importantly, a crudely worked stone font in the monastery itself is said to have been used for washing the pilgrim's feet.

In summer, the path to St Blane's ruined monastery is edged with the pink spires of foxgloves. The coffins borne along it were destined for different cemeteries – the upper one for men, the lower for women. The custom of separate burials survived for 100 years after the Reformation, ending only in 1661.

Blane himself was a pilgrim, following in his uncle's footsteps for much of the time. In the parish of Glen Shira, the churchyard of Kilblaan is described as 'an ancient burying-ground once attached to a sacred building erected by Blane.'[15]

Sailing down Loch Fyne to the Firth of Clyde, Blane is thought to have established a mission on the south shore, near Greenock, at Kilblane. Then crossing the Clyde to Cardross, on the north shore, he built another chapel at Colgrain. From here, striking out in a new direction, he found his way to Loch Lomond and from there travelled up the valley of the Endrick to the tributary of the river to which he gave his name.

At the head of the valley, beneath the shelter of the Campsie Fells, in what is now the village of Strathblane, he made a settlement, which probably included a wooden chapel and a place of refuge for the sick. In 1429, during the reign of James I of Scotland, there are several references to a hospital for the poor here. The royal connection is further demonstrated by the fact that the remains of the king's sister, Mary, wife of Sir William Edmonstone, a local laird, are buried beneath the floor of the present church.[16]

More famously, St Blane erected another church above the River Allan at the appropriately named 'Dunblane'. Here, because of its central location, the primitive little chapel became a centre of pilgrimage before, in the 13th century, it was transformed into the cathedral, which, with some alterations, we know today.

The 11th century tower, which forms the nucleus of the cathedral, housed the shrine of Columba, not the saint of Iona, but the revered companion of St Blane.

St Blane's Chapel on the Island of Bute,
where the saint lived and is thought to have died

St Blane made other foundations in Perthshire. St Blaan's Chapel is near Edinample at the head of Loch Earn. In Inverness-shire, on Loch Shiel, Camas Bhlathain, signifies his name. In Aberdeenshire, Kilblain, near Old Meldrum, means 'church of' or 'cell of Blane'; while Petblane, in the parish of Daviot, means 'Blane's Share'.

This appears to have been the limit of his travels. 'Triumphant Blaan of the Britons' died on 10 August c.590,[17] probably in his monastery of Kingarth, on the island of Bute.

St Fillan
of the Miracles

L ike that of St Maelrubha, the legendary life of St Fillan is difficult to trace on account of there being two saints of the same name. The best known was the son of the Irish princess, St Kentigerna. A daughter of Cellach Cualann, King of Leinster, St Kentigerna married Faradach (Prince of Monchestree of the race of Fiatach Finn) and had numerous children, the most famous of whom was St Fillan. St Kentigerna died on the island of Inchcailleach ('island of the old woman') on Loch Lomond, where the ruined church is said to be have been founded on the site of her cell.

Her son, Fillan, having been instructed by his uncle, St Comgan, moved to the borders of Perthshire and Argyll. He gave his name to Strathfillan, where, beside the river which is the headwater of the Tay, he built his own primitive cell.

This part of Scotland (between Tyndrum and Crianlarich) was then very wild. St Fillan is said to have driven a ferocious boar from the glen. Another fable tells how a wolf, which had killed and eaten one of his oxen, became so tame that he harnessed it to a cart which carried the stones used to build the chapel.

This little building – more probably made of wood – stood on the site of the ruins of the later priory of St Fillan. Significantly, the graveyard is on the north side in accordance with the custom of the old Celtic church. Later, following its affiliation with Rome, burial grounds were sited invariably to the south and west of the church itself.

A short way up the river, above the site of the priory, is the Holy Pool of St Fillan. It was believed to hold the cure for lunacy, as well as other ills. Perhaps the water, which in spring foams down from the snow-covered heights of Ben Oss and Ben Challum, was cold enough to shock the system. In the early 19th century, Sir Walter Scott wrote of how:

> *St Fillan's blessed well*
> *Whose spring can frenzied dreams dispel,*
> *And the crazed brain restore*

Certainly, it was still famous in the early 1700s when Rob Roy MacGregor reputedly ducked a miscreant who had taken another man's land.

St Fillan was so greatly venerated that his relics were kept by five hereditary 'Dewars', [18] each of whom had a croft of land in perpetuity for guarding them. Most famous of these relics is the Quigrich, the head of the saint's pastoral staff, which is one of the wonderful examples of intricate Celtic art. Having been back and forth to Canada over the years, it is now in the National Museum in Edinburgh. So is the Bername, a cast bronze bell which was once placed on the heads of mad people (who were strapped down) to aid their cure.

A relic now vanished is the 'mayne', the forearm and hand of the saint's left arm which was said to give forth a brilliant light while Fillan wrote with his right hand.

This mummified limb, encased in silver, was taken, together with other relics (including pieces of St Andrew's bone) to King Robert the Bruce before the Battle of Bannockburn. Later, in gratitude for the victory which he attributed to the arm's miraculous power, the king founded the now ruined Priory of St Fillan on the site of the saint's early cell.

On 26th February 1317/18, Robert I granted the patronage of the church of Killin to Inchaffray Abbey so that this

house might provide a canon to
celebrate divine service in the church
of Strathfillan.[19]

A glance at the map proves its importance as
a pilgrim route. The original track through
Strathfillan, now replaced by the A82, has
been a link between the main highways from
north, south, east and west since before
recorded time. One main purpose of the
priory was to provide rest and sustenance to
the pilgrims and other travellers who
followed this old established route.

St Fyndoca

and the Holy Isle of Inishail

Donald, or Donevaldus, was a godly
man who lived in the Glen of
Ogilvie. He had nine daughters, the
third of whom was Fyndoca.

When their father died, they moved to
Abernethy, on the River Tay, where they were
granted protection and given a house by
Garnait, a Pictish ruler, who held sway in the
district from 706 to 729.

At Newburgh, near where they lived, a
spring called Ninewells was named after the
maidens. Criminals washed their hands in the
clear water to clean away their sins before
seeking sanctuary at the once famous

Macduff's Cross, of which only the pedestal now remains.

Findoca became an evangelist. Finding her way from Perthshire to Argyll, she probably travelled by boat up Loch Tay and then through Glendochart and Strathfillan to the watershed near Tyndrum. From there, she went down Glen Lochy to its confluence with the River Orchy, which runs into Loch Awe.

The largest island on that great stretch of inland waterway has been known as Inishail – Gaelic for the 'holy island' – since written records began. Standing below the south slope of the mighty mountain of Cruachan, it is one of the most beautiful and peaceful places on earth, especially in late spring when wild hyacinths stretch like a blue veil above a sunlit loch.

Adomnan, Columba's biographer, says that the saint knew of Loch Awe. Proof other than this relating to his time (he died in 597) cannot be found but undoubtedly the holy island of Inishail was venerated from very early times.

Apparently, the first religious settlers were nuns, presumably followers of St Findoca, who were 'remarkable for the sanctity of their lives and the purety of their manners'.[20]

The cross-decorated slab, originally in the graveyard, now standing within the ruined church, is thought to date from the 9th century. However, the first record of the church is in 1257, when Ath, son of Malcolm MacNachtan, granted the 'teinds', or tithes, of 'the church of St Findoca of Inchealt' to the Augustinian canons of Inchaffray Abbey.'[21]

The now ruined church, originally the Parish Church of Inishail, was replaced by a newer building (which is said to have been taken stone by stone from the island) sited by the shore at Cladich *c*.1736.

Inishail has long been a magnet for pilgrims. Glen Aray is *Gleann Aorabh* in Gaelic and means 'Glen of Worship'. Pilgrims heading north from Inveraray ascended the track from Loch Fyne along the River Aray. Trudging slowly through moorland as the path grew steeper to the head of the glen, they suddenly reach the summit of the pass to find themselves looking down on Loch Awe.

Today, the view remains heart stopping, especially on a clear, still day when the island, now covered with trees, floats like a mirage on water that reflects the seven peaks of Cruachan. The pilgrims, knowing they were in sight of their goal, were overjoyed and flung themselves down in veneration at the spot where the Cross of Prostration once stood.[22] Known later as the 'Kneeling Stone', it is now almost impossible to identify this rock.

From the hill, the Christians hastened downwards to the south-east shore of Loch Awe to be ferried across to the island they had come so many weary miles to find.

Although ferries no longer ply on a regular basis across Loch Awe, boats are available for hire so that people can still visit the pilgrim's isle.

ST DUTHAC

and the Royal Road to Tain

King James IV of Scotland was obsessed with guilt which never could be assuaged. As a boy of 15 he had fought with the enemies of his father, James III, at Sauchieburn where the king, thrown from his bolting grey stallion, had been stabbed to death by an impostor claiming to be a priest.

Ever since then, James, overcome with remorse, had worn a chastity belt to which he constantly added more weight. Despite this, he suffered from bouts of deep despondency which only physical exercise, in particular long hours in the saddle on the most mettlesome horse he could find, would disperse.

Urged on by his conscience, the king rode hard, driving out the demons by spurring his horse's sides. Most frequently, he went to Whithorn, but almost every year in the autumn, and sometimes also in spring, he followed his father's footsteps by travelling up the east coast to the little town of Tain.

The devotion of James IV to the shrine of St Duthac is surprising in view of the fact that, even in his time, the dates of the saint's life-span were vague. Duthac is believed to have been born sometime in the early 11th century in Tain in the now roofless chapel on the site of the Chapter House.[23] The chapel was burnt down in a fight between the Mowats and the MacNeills in 1427 when the turf roof caught fire.

Duthac's parents were of high rank. He 'sprang from no ignoble family in Scotland' and they sent him to Ireland to be educated in one of the monastic houses which had the best teachers of those times. Vowing to be a missionary, he returned to Ross-shire where, thanks both to intellectual ability, and perhaps partly to nepotism, he soon became a bishop in the Roman Catholic church

He is claimed to have travelled along the coast of the Moray Firth to Nairn, Forres, and then to Stonehaven on the North Sea where nearby Arduthie is attributed to his name. In Fife, Baldutho means 'Duthac's Town' and in Perthshire the parish of Newburgh was dedicated to St Duthac.

Travelling west from Tain, he established the 'Church of Kilduich' at the head of Loch Duich in Kintail. Likewise, Cadha Dhubhthaich, or 'Duthac's path', is the pass leading from the River Conag to Glen Affric.

In Caithness, the chapel of St Duthac at Wick, known as the Kirk of Moss or 'St Dudoch's Kirk', was reached by a causeway across a bog. His memory here was perpetuated by the offerings of bread and cheese and even silver left on a stone on Christmas morning.

The Pentland Firth is notoriously dangerous but over it went Duthac in his coracle of hides. In Orkney, he built a chapel

Old St Duthus Church, Tain, built around 1360

at Pickaquoy in Kirkwall, and a place at Tensten, in South Sandwick, was called 'St Duthais Hows' (or 'house').

When, in the 14th century, the Sinclair earls came to Orkney from the north of Scotland, they brought with them their family dedication to St Duthac. William Sinclair, Earl of Orkney, founded a chapel in Kirkwall, dedicated to St Duthac, at about that time.

Duthac, reputed to have had second sight, apparently worked miracles. As a young man he carried burning thorns under his shirt which scorched neither skin or clothes. Later he made a cake of butter and honey which cured sickness.[24]

St Duthac's shirt was a treasured relic in the Middle Ages. By then his fame had resulted in Tain being called *Baile-Dhuich*, 'Duthac's Town'. St Duthac's Fair was at one time a great annual event which drew people from far and wide.

The date of his death is uncertain. One source claims that he died in Ireland on 8 March 1065. According to this, his body was brought home to Tain and, seven years later, when disinterred, it showed no sign of decomposition. Both his head and breastbone were kept as relics, suggesting that his corpse had been embalmed. Later records aver that he died almost 200 years later, in 1253 (*Camerarius*) and 1249 (*Acta Sanctorum*).[25]

The date of Duthac's canonisation is unrecorded but, following his death, the sanctuary of the girth of Tain evolved. The burgh came under the special protection of the Holy See, when immunity from paying taxes was granted by Malcolm III to all the citizens and their goods.

The original chapel, burnt in 1427, was repaired but a larger church was needed as the population grew. In 1321, a full collegiate establishment was founded by William, Earl of Ross, who was granted a charter by King Robert the Bruce 'to found and endow six chaplainries in the chapel of St Duthac of Tain, for the saying of masses for the souls of Alexander III and of John, Duke of Atholl . . . and for the souls of all Christian people.'

In 1487, a Charter of Confirmation was given to Thomas, Bishop of Ross, for the foundation of the Collegiate Kirk of St Duthac of Tain, and in 1492 the foundation received Papal Confirmation.

From that time onwards, the little town in Ross-shire, already a venue for pilgrims, became even better known. In 1503, when King James IV came to Tain, tragedy had again overwhelmed him. Only two years before, his mistress, Margaret Drummond, had died from eating poisoned meat sent secretly by men who feared that the king would renege on his arranged marriage to Margaret Tudor, sister of King Henry VIII.

James usually spent the last night of his journey to Tain at Inverness or at Cromarty from where he was ferried across the Cromarty Firth. In 1504, he went again, this time walking barefoot along the moorland tracks (thereafter known as the 'King's Causeway') to make offerings at both 'St Dutho's chapell where he was born and in St Dutho's chapell in the kirkyard of Tayn'.

During another visit in 1506, the king gave money to several people, including the man who carried the saint's bell on ceremonial occasions. Later, in 1511, he paid the royal embroiderers to repair the saint's sark (shirt) and instructed John Edmonstone,

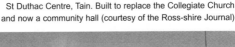

St Duthac Centre, Tain. Built to replace the Collegiate Church and now a community hall (courtesy of the Ross-shire Journal)

keeper of the silver vessels, to send John Aitken, the goldsmith, 'ane of the auld silver plates, broken', containing around 23 ounces of silver, to be melted down and re-fashioned as a reliquary for St Duthac.

This was his last visit. Two years later, at the Battle of Flodden, James IV was killed. His son, James V, also visited Tain but not with his father's zeal. Nonetheless, prior to the Reformation of 1560, the shrine of St Duthac remained a venue for pilgrims who traversed the long miles on horseback or on foot, or else came over the sea, to the little town in Ross-shire, from where the saint himself, on his missionary journeys, had travelled so far and wide.

The King's Causeway is said to have been built by the people of Tain for James IV when they heard that he was making a barefoot pilgrimage to the shrine of St Duthac. Most of the line followed by the causeway is now occupied by a more modern road, but part of the original road (shown below) was left out at a bend, the new one taking a straighter course (courtesy of Tain and District Museum)

SHRINES OF THE
FORTH VALLEY & TAY

LOCH LEVEN
Priory of St Serf

O n an island in the south-east end of Loch Leven in Kinross stands one of the oldest religious foundations in Scotland. For centuries a place of pilgrimage, it is attributed to St Serf. The saint is a legendary figure whose history is much confused because there appears to have been two men of the same name.

The first lived in AD500, the second some 200 years later. A 13th-century manuscript – now in Dublin, but probably originally kept in Glasgow Cathedral – is a copy of Jocelin of Furness's *Vita Sancti Kentigerni*, in which, because of his supposed connection with St Kentigern, patron saint of Glasgow, a *Vita Sancti Servani* (biography of St Serf) is included. St Serf is reputed to have rescued the infant Kentigern after his mother, turned out by her cruel father, had drifted to Culross in a coracle (*see page 44*).

The story reads like a fairy tale. It claims that St Serf's father was a king of Canaan and his mother a princess of Arabia. They had two sons of whom the eldest, Servanus (Serf), chose to become a monk and a priest. He went to Jerusalem, Constantinople, and then to Rome, where he was immediately elected Pope. Seven years later he left Rome and headed north. Struggling against violent snow storms, he believed that the elements had changed into demons who sought to prevent him crossing the high passes in the Alps. Undeterred, St Serf's journey eventually took him over the English Channel and into the Firth of Forth.

Andrew de Wyntoun, one of the earliest Scottish historians, who was prior in the early 15th century, wrote in his *Origynale Cronykil* of the man who came to Scotland *c.*690. He goes on to describe how this man – St Serf – set sail with 100 companions and commanded the wind to carry them whether it would. It brought them to the Firth of Forth and they landed at Inchkeith.

There he was met by St Adomnan, decribed as 'abbot in Scotland at that time'. Adomnan is said to have given him 'the land of Fife from the hill of the Britons to the Ochil hills for his familia'.[1]

Adomnan, biographer of Columba, lived from *c.*625–704. The Pictish King Brude, *Bruide mac Derileu ri Cruithintuathi* was converted to Christianity by Columba and was one of Adomnan's guarantors.[2]

Nonetheless, when St Serf and his companions started to clear the undergrowth at Culross on the north shore of the Firth of Forth – Culross (*cuilen ros*), means 'holly point' – for their settlement, they were attacked by King Brude's son. However, when the king himself was saved from a mysterious illness by the prayers of St Serf, he granted Culross, once and for all, to the saint. Later, according to this account, Adomnan gave St Serf Loch Leven and the island on which he lived for seven years.

St Serf also had a cell at Dunning in Perthshire, at the foot of the Ochills. Nearby, in a place once called *Vallis Draconis*, he is said to have slain a dragon, which had terrorised the district, with his pastoral staff. Another of his retreats was a cave at Dysart, on the north shore of the Firth of Forth, for long a great venue of pilgrims. Here, he famously had a contest with the devil, whom he overcame.

St Serf is said to have died at Dunning, in extreme old age, on the first day of the kalends (kalends meaning 'month' in the ancient Roman calendar) of July in 543.

The island on Loch Leven, in Fife, which was given to St Serf, was originally the site of a Culdee, or Celtic foundation. The 'Culdees' or *Celedei*, 'Servants of God', belonged to the order of Christian monks who came mainly from Ireland and established settlements on the West of Scotland and Wales in the 6th and 7th centuries. They abided by the rules of their monastic order, known as Canon Law. The Culdees are known to have founded a settlement in Loch Leven in 838 on the site of the original Celtic foundation.

The introduction of feudalism in the early 12th century led to King David I granting the island to the Augustine Catholics of St Andrews *c*.1150. Shortly afterwards, in 1152, the priory (as it now was), became a subsidiary of St Andrews.[3]

In 1396, Andrew de Wyntoun became prior of the monastery on St Serf's Island in Loch Leven. Then, some 70 years later, Walter Monypenny became prior on 22 September 1465. The fact that by this time the priory is frequently called 'St Serf's' or 'Portmook' suggests that the monks may by then have been living both on the island and at Portmoak on the nearby shore of the loch.[4] Certainly, a hospital, located 'at the bridge of Portmak' which was 'for the reception of poor people,' was in existence as early as 1184.

A church, dedicated to St Mary, had replaced the original chapel of the culdees. The priory on St Serf's Island survived the Reformation and was still in use in 1567 when Mary Queen of Scots was imprisoned in the castle on another nearby island. We do not know if the unfortunate queen was allowed to visit it by boat, but the sound of the bells tolling for vespers must, on still days, have reached her across the water and possibly brought her some comfort at a time of great distress.

A charter of Queen Mary's son King James VI & I, dated 29 July 1580, granted the priory of Portmoak to St Leonard's College, St Andrews.[5]

Pilgrims have travelled to Loch Leven from the time of the first religious settlement on the island sometime around AD700. The loch was within walking distance from the Firth of Tay to the north, and the Firth of Forth to the south. Reaching the shore of the loch, pilgrims would have been ferried to the priory on the island by one of the local boatmen who jealously guarded their rights concerning this lucrative trade. Even today, many still make the boat journey to the now ruined priory.

INCHCOLM

Retreat of St Colm

The island of Inchcolm lies in the Firth of Forth off the coast of Fife. It is believed to take its name from St Colm, a disciple of St Drostan, who lived in the latter part of the 6th century. A hill four miles inland from Inchcolm is called Pitcolme and, because of the prefix being Pictish, it is taken that St Colm was a Pict.

Inchcolm, the island in the Firth of Forth where
St Colm built a primitive cell as his retreat

St Colm built a primitive bee-hive roofed
cell on the island of his retreat. According to
the historian Hector Boece, the island was
much venerated in the 11th century. The
Danes paid large sums to be buried there and
it has long been a place of refuge for sailors
when gales blow up the Forth.

In 1123, a fierce storm attacked the ship of
Alexander I. Fearing for his life, the king
prayed to St Columba to save him and he
landed safely on Inchcolm, where he was
storm-bound for three days. On the island he
found a hermit, living alone in his cell and
existing entirely on shellfish and the milk of a
cow. As he shared what he had with the king,
the anchorite told him how he lived by the

rules of St Columba. Later, Alexander, in gratitude for his escape, founded a priory of Augustinian Canons on the island which he dedicated to St Columba.

The priory became an abbey on 21 May 1235. It is said to have been attacked by the English, first in 1335 and again in 1385, by which time many of the monks had fled in terror to the mainland. Walter Bower, writer of the Scottish history *Scotichronicon*, was Abbot of Inchcolm *c*.1420. His dream was to make Inchcolm a centre of ecclesiastical learning modelled on that on Iona.

It was during his time that enlargement and restoration of the abbey began. Following the Reformation, the abbey and its lands were made into a temporal lordship for Henry Stewart, Lord St Colme, by the parliament of 1609. The Earl of Moray, descendant of Lord St Colme, gave the buildings to the care of the government in 1924. Sadly, the abbey has suffered at the hands of time and of the original buildings only the tower now remains.

The island of Inchcolm again became a focal point during the two World Wars. The concrete blocks on which guns and searchlights were mounted remain in proof of the occupation of the armed forces who helped to guard the many naval vessels, including troopships and aircraft carriers, as well as the countless merchant vessels which sailed through the vitally important waterway of the estuary of the Forth.

THE BASS ROCK
St Baldred's Isle

T he Bass Rock is one of the best-known landmarks of the Firth of Forth. An ancient volcanic structure, rising to a height of 313 feet, it juts from the sea off the point of Tantallon about a mile from North Berwick. Now deserted except for its colony of gannets which, during the breeding season, rise screaming at a boat's approach, it was once the place that the hermit St Baldred chose as his retreat.

St Baldred, described as 'an Anglic anchorite' was a missionary from the Romanised See of Lindisfarne to which East Lothian (then politically part of Northumbria), was ecclesiastically attached.[6] In the early part of the 8th century, the Bass Rock was just as forbidding as it is today. Sheer precipices plunge to the sea and it is almost impossible to land, apart from one point on the south where, except in the roughest weather, you can scramble ashore.

St Baldred, from his rock-bound fastness, crossed repeatedly to the mainland to preach to the local people. The parish of Tyningham is frequently mentioned as a place of his ministry. The foundation of the monastery at Tyningham, at the mouth of the River Tyne, is attributed to 'Balthere the anchorite', popularly known in the district as 'St Baldred of the Bass.'

The Parish Church of Prestonkirk is believed to stand on the site of a chapel which he built. Nearby St Baldred's Well was a place of pilgrimage for those sick in mind and body who came to drink its ice cold water, believing it could cure all ills.

Simeon of Durham, in his *History of the Kings*, records the death of St Baldred 'in Tiningaham' (Tyninghame), near Dunbar, in 756.

Later, a church was built upon the site of the saint's primitive cell on the Bass Rock. In February 1406, Sir David Fleming, King Robert III's faithful retainer, took the young Prince James – the king's only surviving son, whose life was endangered by his ambitious relations – to North Berwick. There he found a boat in which the young James was 'rowyt to the Bass',[7] proving that people were then ferried to the island in much the same way as today.

Prince James spent a month on the Bass, waiting with his escort for a ship to take them to France. He probably lived largely on salted gannets which the monks provided. Catching these birds was no easy task – the monks had to descend the sheer cliff face on ropes to steal the young birds from their nests.

Incarcerated in a cold smoky building, roofed with turf, the prince must have been thankful when the sails of the *Marienknight* of Danzig finally came within sight.

His eagerness was soon turned to misery, however, as he was captured off Flamburgh

Head by pirates who took him as a prisoner to the English King Henry IV.

No doubt the church suffered from the extreme conditions of its site, because in 1542, under the direction of Cardinal Beaton, the old church on the Bass was rebuilt. Dedicated to St Baldred, the stones of his cell were used to build the church walls.[8]

The monks, marooned for long periods during storms, had a hard life. In calm weather, supplies could be landed, including the precious bear or barley, used for brewing ale. Pilgrims may have brought gifts with them when they came by boat from North Berwick. The loneliness would also have been alievated by the prisoners who, it is said, were sometimes rescued by the monks. These unfortunates would have been cast adrift

The forbidding Bass Rock, where
St Baldred once lived in his hermit's cell

from the dungeon of the Douglas fortress of Tantallon, which stands high upon the cliffs on the nearby mainland shore.

The village of Earlsferry in Fife gained its name from the ferry which carried passengers to and from North Berwick in early medieval times. An old legend tells that MacDuff, Earl of Fife, hid from Macbeth (the tyrant of Shakespeare's play) in a cave near the village, until he was rescued by local fishermen who took him to safety across the Firth.

The Auld Kirk at North Berwick once stood on a tidal peninsula, connected to the shore by an arched bridge. Built during the 12th century, the remains have recently been re-excavated. Dedicated to St Andrew, it was greatly significant as a staging post for the pilgrims, en route to St Andrews, who crossed the Firth of Forth on the Earl's ferry to reach the Fife shore.

A stone mould for the manufacture of pilgrim's badges was dug up on the Kirk Green at North Berwick in the 19th century. Bearing a rude likeness of St Andrew on his diagonal cross, it is thought to be from the 13th or 14th century.

A house of Cistercian nuns was also founded at North Berwick in the 12th century. Pilgrims could worship here before embarking on what was frequently a dangerous journey across the Firth of Forth. The nuns, who issued the badges, managed the business side of a lucrative trade as the ferry plied back and forth to Fife.[9]

This was one of the pilgrimages to which much spiritual value was attached. The longer and more hazardous the journey, the greater the expurgation of the sin.

A famous ghost story relates to the Royal Hotel in North Berwick which, until recently, stood beside the railway station below North Berwick Law. On a still summer night not long ago, two men of highly reputable standing maintained that they clearly heard the monks singing on the Bass, years after the last of them had died. Perhaps the voices of those living in a fastness, dedicated to the love of God, may still linger in sound waves which survive the passing of time.

Icon of St Adrian of May
(courtesy of Brother Adrian,
Pluscarden Abbey)

THE ISLE OF MAY
Eternal Light of St Adrian

Still farther east, in the Firth of Forth, five miles from the coast of Fife, lies the Isle of May, which was to become associated with another saint.

Ethernan, whose name in Latin means 'eternal', is more commonly known as St Adrian. The old legend that he came

124

from Hungary, purported by the *Aberdeen Breviary*, is now largely dismissed. His origins are now generally accepted as Pictish. Like Columba, he is said to have been the son of noble parents and, after being sent to study in Ireland, he returned to Scotland *c.*650. With him came a band of monks with whom he spread the faith of the gospels in the east coast of Scotland.

Like many Christians before and after him, St Adrian sought a heavenly reward in return for living a life of abstinence, the subjugation of carnal lusts and by renouncing the temptations of the world.

So St Adrian, like Columba, left his noble family and moved to the Isle of May. There he built a primitive chapel where a small religious community survived on what they could grow and on the milk of their few cows. They also offered sanctuary to seamen who were wrecked upon the island's rocky shores. In later times the monks who dwelt on the island burnt a light – forerunner to the modern-day lighthouse – to warn vessels of danger.

The records of the Priory of St Andrews mention 'the light of St Ethernan [St Adrian] on the Isle of May'and also tell of how the Earl of Buchan gave the monks a stone of wax, far better than tallow for making candles, or an annual donation of 40 pence.

Sadly, the peaceful life of the small Christian community was brutally destroyed by Viking raiders. It is known that, in about

870, a large party of Danes invaded the east coast of Scotland, where they killed and pillaged without mercy. The *Aberdeen Breviary* says that they came to the Isle of May and murdered St Adrian and all his monks.

Wyntoun, the prior of Loch Leven, describes how:

> *Saynt Adriane they slewe in May*
> *Wyth mony of hys company.*

He also affirms that this happened when Constantine, son of Kenneth MacAlpin, ruled over Scotland from 863–876. Therefore it seems that St Adrian and his companions arrived at the time when the Scots were driving the Picts from their ancient lands and that they themselves were then killed on the Isle of May by the Danes.

During recent excavations on the island, a large number of what appear to be Christian burials, dating from the 5th to the 10th centuries, have been found beneath a cairn and in two 'long-cist' cemeteries (tombs consisting of rows of stones on edge, covered with rough slabs).[10]

The Isle of May, described as 'the gift of David I' was confirmed to the English Abbey of Reading by Pope Alexander III (1119–81). Then, in a charter of William the Lion (–1219), it is stated that the king confirms the priory's possessions 'so that a convent of 13 monks of the Cluniac order may be maintained there'. Later the convent became Benedictine.

In 1292/3, the Abbot of Reading petitioned the Scottish king (John Balliol) and his parliament to the effect that the priory of May had been illegally sold by one Robert de Burghgate to William (Fraser), Bishop of St Andrews, for £1,000. The Abbot of Reading claimed that the deal was illegal on the grounds that the Bishop of St Andrews, as a guardian of the realm of Scotland, was sworn to maintain the royal patrimony. Therefore he had no right to treat with Burghgate and, since Burghgate had acted without the consent of his convent, he was deposed.

Subsequently, inspired by the story of St Adrian's martyrdom, the Isle of May had become a magnet for pilgrims by the 15th century. An affiliation with the Cathedral of Santiago de Compostela was discovered by Peter Yeoman, Council Archaeologist for Fife, who, when carrying out extensive excavations, found a skeleton with the pilgrim's badge of a scallop shell wedged between the teeth.

The scallop shell was associated with St James (whose remains are said to be buried in the Spanish Cathedral) because of an old legend which tells of how the sailors of the ship which was carrying his remains to Spain rescued a horse and rider from drowning, the bodies of both being curiously covered with such shells (see p.31).

Royal patronage cemented the Isle's reputation as a holy place when, in the early 1500s, King James IV of Scotland, together with Queen Margaret, made several pilgrimages there. In 1503, the whole choir of the Chapel Royal in Stirling was taken on one of the king's own ships to sing a mass on the island. The monastery was now much ruined but a small chapel and a pilgrim's hostel still stood within the west range of the priory.

A hermit, who acted as a caretaker, survived to a large extent on the rabbits, which having been introduced to the island, throve in the absence of foxes.

Following James IV's death at the battle of Flodden in 1513, the priory, already dilapidated, fell into even greater disrepair and the monks had long since moved to Pittenweem.

'On 30 January 1549/50 the Prior of Pittenweem granted a lease of the Isle of May, which is said to be now lying waste.'[11]

Ten years later the Presbyterian leaders of the Reformation declaimed pilgrimage as idolatrous. Nonetheless, people still came secretly to the Isle of May, sailing under cover of darkness from the fishing villages on the coast.

Landing, they prayed to St Adrian and drank water – supposed to be specially efficacious for barren women – from the famous St Adrian's Well. The holy well, so significant of the faith of those who sought salvation, remains at Pilgrim's Haven, near to where the monks originally landed, to the present day. Sadly, however, only the shell of their chapel survives.

St Mary's, Whitekirk
The Barefoot Pilgrim

By the early 1300s, in the days of King Robert the Bruce, the healing powers of the water of St Mary's Well at Whitekirk brought pilgrims from far and wide. By all accounts, there were so many miracles performed at this well that, in 1309, John Abernethy (with the assistance of the monks at Melrose), procured a shrine to be erected and dedicated to the Holy Mother. The shrine was sited in the church, near which, in a field some 200 metres to the east, stands the Holy Well.

The Church of St Mary at Whitekirk (or 'Fairknowe', as it was first called) is known to have been in existence by 1356, at the time of Edward III's invasion of Scotland. Some of his soldiers broke into the sanctuary and stole the jewels adorning the image of the Virgin.

They soon met their fate. Fordoun says that a disastrous storm arose and 'the ship which had wrought the heinous robbery, and its crew which had dared to lay hands on The Lady of the World, where whelmed in the gulf of the deep in the sight of many.'

The statue itself, described by the historians Gibbon and Ross as occupying a niche above the 'square headed'[12] door, subsequently disappeared.

So great was the attraction of the church itself and of the nearby well that, in 1413, there were no less than 15,653 pilgrims of all nations and the annual offerings were equal to 1,422 merks.[13]

In 1430, James I, King of Scotland, being a religious man who loved the Church, took the chapel of Fairknowe into his protection. He added to it by building houses for the protection of pilgrims, called it the White Chapel and apparently was a frequent member of the congregation.'[14]

At the time, the Scottish Church was under the auspices of Rome, and many church officials exploited the fact that they were removed from authority. Rumours of their misdeeds reached the Papal Court and Pope Eugenius IV decided to send a nuncio to investigate. So in 1435, in the 11th year of King James's reign, Aeneas Sylvius set forth for the Scottish court to carry out his mission.

The envoy's journey was delayed. It was late autumn before he set sail from Sluys across the North Sea. A violent storm blew up and his ship was driven to Norway before the gale. Thinking that his last hour had come, he prayed for deliverance, swearing that he would walk barefoot to the nearest church were his life to be spared. His plea was granted, the wind abated and, at Aberlady, he thankfully came ashore.

To his dismay, he found that the nearest shrine was at Whitekirk, at least ten miles away. But his word was pledged; he had to keep his vow. Stumbling and slipping on the snow-covered, frozen ground, the unfortunate Italian may well have wished that he had drowned after all.

Somehow, supported by his monks, he limped to St Mary's Church where, once within its sanctuary, he collapsed. His feet were so badly frost-bitten that he had to rest for two days before he had recovered enough to be carried onwards to the king. Aeneas Sylvius did return to Italy (where 20 years later, he became Pope Pius II) but, thanks to his ordeal in Scotland, he remained crippled by rheumatism for the rest of his life.[15]

Today, an annual pilgrimage takes place from St Mary's Church at Whitekirk to St Mary's Church at Haddington in remembrance of the Pope's nuncio. Nowadays, however, the path is devoid of the hazards which beset him.

St Mary's Church, Whitekirk, where every year, on the second Saturday in May, pilgrims from far and near still congregate (courtesy of Brian Pugh)

St Mary's, Haddington
The Lamp of Lothian

The Cistercian Order, also called the White Monks on account of their wearing a habit made of undyed wool, was founded in 1098 and followed an especially strict form of the Benedictine rule.

In 1159, a nunnery of the Cistercian order was founded in Haddington by Ada, Countess of Northumberland and Huntingdon. At that time, East Lothian (where Haddington lies) was part of Northumbria.

One of the largest in Scotland, the nunnery is said to have housed 24 nuns. The prioresses swore fealty to Edward I of England in 1291 and 1296.

Nonetheless, their house was burned by the English in February 1335 or 1366 and again in May 1534. Following the Reformation, parliament decreed that the nunnery be erected into a temporal lordship (property belonging to a layman) for John Maitland, master of Lauderdale, in 1621.

The Greyfriars came to Haddington shortly after the death of their founder St Francis of Assisi. The church that they built by the River Tyne became known as the 'Lamp of Lothian' because of the 'elegance and clearness of light in its choir'.

The Greyfriars Church of Haddington is first mentioned in *The Chronicle of Lanercost*

St Mary's Church, Haddington, 'The Lamp of Lothian'

which records that Patrick, Earl of Athole, was buried there in 1242. The historian John Major, the first to call the church the 'Lamp of Lothian', testifies that, together with the nunnery, it was burned by the English in 1355.

The church was not a grand edifice but a simple building. Even so, because of the goodness of its monks, it drew people to its doors, like moths to a candle. By the time of its destruction there must have been a hospital where the friars, poor as they were themselves, cared for the sick and the destitute. It is known that they also sheltered people suffering from leprosy, a disease very common at that time.

The hospital, largely due to the destruction of the English, fell into disrepair and had to be rebuilt. The Haddington Burgh Writs record that 'in terms of the refoundation of St Laurence's hospital, 1470–2, a chalder of victual [barley, oats or malt] is to be given to its master, at the two yearly terms, to the lepers of Haddington, dwelling in the leper house.'[16]

Previous to this, in 1380, work had begun on St Mary's, a short way from the friary church. The new building was one of the three great pre-Reformation churches of the Lothians: the others being St Giles in Edinburgh (*see page 137*) and St Michael's in Linlithgow.

In June 1478, the Greyfriars of Haddingon and John Haliburton, vicar of Greenlaw, erected an almshouse in the 'Poldrait (neighbourhood) of Haddington'.

The friars were shown no mercy despite the sanctity of their work. In 1544, the church was again sacked by the English. This time there is no mention of restoration – perhaps the cost was too high – and in 1572 the Town Council ordered that the Friar's church should be demolished.

In 1548, during the war between Henry VIII of England and the Scottish Regency, St Mary's was almost destroyed by the English army. However, following the Restoration, at the request of John Knox, who was born in Haddington, the nave was re-roofed and repaired. A wall was also built to divide it from the rest of the ruined building and it remained the Parish Church for 400 years.

The choir and the transepts were left in ruin until, in the early 1970s, a major programme of restoration began. The work was so skilfully executed that now it is difficult to discern between the old fabric and the new. The ceiling of the choir, which appears to be constructed in the same way as that of the nave, is actually made of fibreglass, thanks to the boat-building technology of the 1970s.

Equally amazing is the fact that the beautiful stained-glass window in the South Transept actually came from St Michael's Church in Torquay. After they had been taken from there, the glass panes were stored in boxes in the Victoria and Albert Museum during the 1930s. Then, almost miraculously, they were found to be the right size for the wall space in St Mary's which needed to be filled.

Mysterious medieval carvings around the church include images of Green Men and scallop shells, so long the insignia of pilgrims. Within the church itself, the Lauderdale Aisle is an Episcopal chapel within a Church of Scotland building. Since the Episcopal religion is governed by a bishop and the Church of Scotland is ruled by moderators, this near unique arrangement, with its strong Catholic and Orthodox influences, represents a bridging of the main differences between the established Church of England and Scotland.

The annual Whitekirk and Haddington Pilgrimage inspired the international pilgrimage in May 2003 when Catholics and Protestants came together in St Mary's Parish Church in Haddington to pray for World Peace.

St Mary's is the largest parish church in Scotland. Cruciform in shape, it is over 196 feet in length. Above the central crossing, the tower is 90 feet high. Now, once again, the choir, with hand-made glass windows, is imbued with 'its elegance and clearness of light' and it can once more fulfil its legendary status as the Lamp of Lothian. Seen from afar across the low-lying fields of East Lothian, the great church, survivor of so much destruction, rises again in majesty, symbolic of the Christian faith.

The majestic St Mary's, Haddington, where pilgrims still follow the old paths (courtesy of Angus Ferguson)

ST GILES CATHEDRAL, EDINBURGH
Dedicated to the Greek Hermit

In 1243, the Romanesque church in the High Street of Edinburgh, built on the site of an earlier foundation, was dedicated to St Giles, patron saint of the town, whose feast day is celebrated on 1 September.

The fact that he was chosen, in preference to a Biblical saint, is highly significant of the then growing hostility with England and the Scots affinity to France.

St Giles was born in Greece and, as the son of an aristocratic Athenian family, he is said to have used his fortune to help the poor. To avoid followers and adulation, he left Greece *c.*683 for France, seeking seclusion first in a remote place near the mouth of the Rhone and later by the River Gard in Provence where he lived as a hermit. However, then becoming famed for his sanctity, he attracted so many pilgrims that he withdrew into a dense forest near Nimes where his lifestyle was so impoverished that, legend says, God sent a hind to nourish him with her milk. This hind, his sole companion, is always pictured with him in medieval paintings.

One day, however, the deer was chased by hunters and led them to the hermit's retreat. They took him to their master, King Wamba (or Flavius) reputedly King of the Visigoths, although actually he must have been one of the Franks who had conquered the Visigoths at least a century before. The King wished to load him with honours but the now crippled saint asked only to build a monastery in his valley. Here he trained several disciples and established Benedictine monks. He died, an old man, famed both for his holiness and the miracles he reputedly performed.

Following his death, his cult spread rapidly throughout Europe to the point where pilgrims flocked to his shrine at Marseilles.[17]

Just before departure they were blessed in their own church and given a symbolic staff to help them on their way. Such a one was William Preston, who, in 1455, returned from France with what was said to be the mummified relic of the arm of St Giles which he gave to his own church in Edinburgh.

The iron prick ends of two pilgrim staffs, buried beside their owners, have been found during excavations in the church, which, dating from the time of Alexander I, *c*.1120, is now the great cathedral of Scotland's capital city.[18]

The lantern
and tower of
St Giles Cathedral

HEALING WELLS

W ater, essential to all life and a
primary religious symbol, holds a
special place in the Christian faith.
The Bible, both the Old Testament and the
New, abounds with examples of how and
why it affected the very existence of man. The
earth was cleansed by the flood, in which
Noah was chosen to survive. Christ was
baptized in the River Jordan, He made a
promise of 'living' (in other words 'running')
water to the woman of Samaria. Prophetically,
it is said that 'you will draw water from the
springs of salvation' and the Bible refers to
'the spring of living water, murmuring "come
to the father".'

Today, as throughout the centuries,
children and adults are christened with water
which must always return to the ground.
Water is symbolic of cleansing. Christ washed
the feet of sinners just as pilgrims, on
reaching Iona, immersed their feet in a basin
hollowed out in a stone, before entering the
abbey. Thus, from earliest biblical times,
water was believed to contain properties
which cleansed evil from both the body and
the soul.

St Mary's Well
Culloden

S t Mary's Well, the 'Clootie Well', is near Black Park Farm, just west of the famous battlefield and about a mile from Culloden House. The well is said to be haunted by the ghosts of Highlanders killed at the Battle of Culloden on 16 April 1746.

The estate of Culloden had been acquired by Duncan Forbes, Provost of Inverness, in 1621. The wife of one of his descendents decided that the well would make a good place for a bath and persuaded her husband to build a wall round it to ensure its privacy. Nonetheless, many people continued to leave food, drink and pieces of clothing for the 'little people', or fairies – a common practice at wells – and to make a wish. More recently, they left money which was given to charity.

Again, as at Orton, the favourite time to visit was on the old pagan festival of Beltane, on the first Sunday in May. So popular did the well become that, in 1953, about 30 buses and 300 cars parked nearby.

Sadly, the well is now largely deserted, the footpath overgrown and the 'clooties' mostly discarded kitchen roll and plastic bags. The well itself looks uncared for, although it has a good supply of water from a spring. This water was supposed to be of exceptional purity, hence its efficacy as a cure.[1]

St Triduana's Well
Restalrig, in Midlothian

S t Regulus or, as he is better known, St Rule, came to St Andrews accompanied by several consecrated virgins. Among them was St Triduana of Colosse, a maiden of great beauty with particularly lovely eyes. She settled for a time at Rescobie in Angus, where, at a later date, the church was dedicated to her name.

According to an old legend, Nectanevus, the Pictish ruler of the district, a savage man, paid court to her, enamoured by the beauty of her eyes. Triduana spurned him and fled to Atholl. However, the courtiers of the prince pursued her and when they caught up with her, she asked them 'What does so great a prince desire of a poor virgin dedicated to God?' 'The most excellent beauty of thine eyes,' they replied. Whereupon she pulled out her beautiful eyes, skewered them upon thorns, and sent them off to her admirer.[2]

Afterwards, remaining unmolested, she spent the rest of her life at Restalrig, in Midlothian, where she was buried following her death. As for Nectavenus, or 'Nectan neave', the man who so desired her, he evidently reformed his evil ways. Converted to Christianity, perhaps by the example of the woman he may have truly loved, he retired into a monastery to become 'St Nectan' in his later days.

On the spot where St Triduana's bones were believed to be buried, a church, dedicated to St Margaret, was built during the 12th century. Some 200 years later, *c*.1477, this old foundation was replaced by another, commissioned by the Logans of Restalrig, for King James III of Scotland. The King made it collegiate, after which it was enlarged by his successors, James IV and James V.

St Triduana's Well stands under the roofed stone structure to the right of the main church and was once revered as Scotland's principal healing water source. Water from the well-house was used to treat all forms of eye complaints because people believed that the saint, who had lost her own sight, could heal the blind. During the Middle Ages it became a famous centre for pilgrims who, either groping along on their own or led by others to the shrine, prayed that the ice cold water might miraculously heal their eyes. The poet, Sir David Lyndsay, wrote that people went to 'Sanct Tredwell [as Triduana is also known] to mend their ene'.

After the Reformation of 1560, the First General Assembly ordered that the church at Restalrig, a 'monument of idolatry', should be 'casten down and destroyed'. It remained a ruin for nearly 300 years until, in 1837, it was restored by the Restalrig Friendly Society.

The well-house, however, lay entirely buried until it was somehow discovered in 1906. The restoration work was then carried out by Thomas Ross, under the supervision of

James Francis Stuart, 16th Earl of Moray. The roof and buttresses were renewed so that the medieval stonework has now virtually disappeared.

The building's rescuers, believing that they had found the family vault of the Logans of Restalrig, were surprised and somewhat dumbfounded when the floor continually flooded. It was only after more thorough investigation that they realised that, what they had taken to be the 'family chapel', was in fact, the legendary St Triduana's Well.

Today this ancient site, the venue of so many pilgrims of the past, is safe in the hands of Historic Scotland. The water still flows under the ancient crypt to this day.

St Triduana became so famous as the healer of eye complaints that, even on far-off Papa Westray, in the Orkneys, a now ruined pilgrims' chapel on the east side of the island was dedicated to her name. The track to the chapel was called the Messigate (Mass Road) and until the 19th century pilgrims continued to brave the disapproval of the kirk by coming here and leaving their offerings.[3]

Whether she really travelled north is doubtful, but Kinellar Church, on the south side of the Don in Aberdeenshire, was dedicated to her name. Here, during rebuilding, Pictish symbols were found in the foundations and likewise ruined chapels in both Sutherland and Caithness, where earth-houses and antlers of reindeer testify to Pictish habitation, bear St Triduana's name.[4]

ST MARGARET'S WELL
Holyrood Park, Edinburgh

The well in Holyrood Park, near the Palace of Holyrood House, so greatly resembles St Triduana's Well at nearby Restalrig, that it is believed to have been originally dedicated to the saint of the blind. Described as 'a miniature medieval Gothic masterpiece', St Margaret's Well was removed from its original site between Restalrig and Meadowbank – now marked by a rough boulder – to Holyrood Park in 1860 to make way for St Margaret's Bogie Works, built by the North British Railway.

The well has a story of its own. It is claimed to be the spring beside which King David I, while hunting a 'muckle hart', fell from his horse. As he lay stunned, the stag he was pursuing turned and gored him in the thigh. Fighting for his life, he was holding it off, grappling with its antlers, when a cross appeared. At the sight of it, the beast turned and fled. That night, in 1128, the king was told in a dream to 'make a house for canons[5] devoted to the Cross'. Thus, the Monastery of the Holy Rood (holy cross) was erected near the spring of St Margaret's Well in 1141.

Industry blossomed under the Abbey of Holyrood, which supported farms and a brewery. Today, only blackened ruins remain of the once magnificent abbey – the size of a cathedral – which King David built. The medieval guest house, which adjoined it, was transformed in 1503 into Holyrood Palace by James IV for his bride Margaret Tudor.

Sometime during the 13th century St Anthony's Chapel was built nearby – the ruins of which can be seen on the hill today. Legend has it that this chapel was built as an annex for the knightly order of St Anthony, or Knights Templar (*see page 32*) and it soon became known as a place of pilgrimage.

With such a strong religious element to Holyrood Park, it also became a place of sanctuary, providing safety for criminals and even debtors living within its boundary.

Tradition has it that a spring, named after St Anthony, used to flow under the chapel arches but this dried up in the 17th century and later re-emerged a little further down the slope on which the chapel is sited. On May Day, the youth of both sexes used to come and wash their faces with morning dew and make a wish at this spot.

THE WELLS OF THE NORTH-EAST

Many wells, mostly dedicated to the Virgin Mary, can be found in North-east Scotland. Following the Reformation, in 1560, the members of the presbyteries did all in their power to

The Chapel Well, Orton (*left*) which is sited near St Mary's Chapel (*right*) (courtesy of Father Giles Conacher)

discourage pilgrims from what they decried as the superstitious worship of 'false idols' which included the 'healing wells'.

They were not always successful. At Seggat, in Auchterless parish, where once stood St Mary's Chapel, there was a famous well where 'pilgrims in days of old' drank its water and made an offering. 'The Presbytery of Turriff, aided by the Synod of Aberdeen, exerted themselves in vain to put an end to the custom.' Twice the well was filled up with a cairn of stones on the orders of the Synod, dated 17 April 1649. On both occasions, the well water was emptied and the stones replaced, but all to no avail as it filled up again with water. Nearly 200 years later, old people remembered 'money and other articles being deposited on "Pash Sunday" by those whose superstitious feelings led them to frequent the well in expectation of some benefit to be derived from drinking the water dedicated to the Holy Virgin'.

At Orton, in Rothes parish near Elgin, in

Morayshire, there was once a chapel
dedicated to St Mary. Nearby was the Chapel
Well which used to be much visited by people
seeking a cure from its waters, particularly on
1 May, this being the old Celtic festival of
Beltane.

Elsewhere throughout Scotland wells
dedicated to St Mary, and to many other
saints, can still be found. The fact that so
many people clung to their belief in the
health-giving powers of the water may be
connected with its purity at a time when
pollution was the cause of much illness and
death. Also, the minerals contained in spring
water may have been efficacious when,
thanks to their poor diet, so many people in
Scotland suffered from numerous ailments;
bad eyesight, in particular, being directly
attributed to this cause.

WELL OF GRACE
by the River Spey

In the ancient parish of Dunurcas, beside
the River Spey, was the Chapel of Grace,
with the Well of Grace beside it. The
chapel was a celebrated pilgrimage centre
even in post-Reformation times. The *Domestic
Annals of Scotland* record that 'one of the chief
places in vogue was the Chapel of Grace, on
the western bank of the Spey, near

Fochabers – a mere ruin, but held in great veneration, and resorted to by devout people from all parts of the north of Scotland'.

We hear of Lady Aboyne travelling to the Chapel of Grace every year – a journey of 30 Scottish miles, the last two of which she always performed on her bare feet.

About the time of the National Covenant (1638) what remained of the Chapel of Grace was torn down, with a view to putting a stop to the pilgrimages, but this seems to have been far from an effectual measure.

Two years previously, a vigorous attempt had been made by the Presbytery of Strathbogie to discountenance such visits to the chapel. In extracts from the *Presbytery Book of Strathbogie* we read: 'At Inverkeithny, September 14, 1636, Peter Wat, summoned to this day for goeing in pilgrimage to the chappell beyond the water of Spey, compeared and confessed his fault. Ordained to make his repentance, and to paye four marks penaltye.

'Agnes Jack summoned to this day for goeing in pilgrimage to the same chappell, compeared, and confessed that she went to the said chappell with ane diseased woman, but gave her great oath that she used no kind of superstitious worship. She is ordained to make her publike repentance, and to abstaine from the lyke in tyme comeing.'[6]

Onwards to the Great Abbeys & Cathedrals

The Monk's Road heads south from the Threipmuir Reservoir just outside Balerno, in Midlothian. From there it continues south to the village of Nine Mile Burn, about nine miles from Edinburgh, just to the north of the A702 trunk road to Edinburgh and Carlisle. From there it continues over open moorland to the top of West Kip, one of the Pentland Hills, with a narrow, rocky summit (551m high) that is gained by a steep, though short, scramble from both sides.

Another route, which follows the broad ridge up Monk's Rig, past the Font Stone, leads up to the top of West Kip before heading down towards the Borders, a track once worn down by the feet of monks and pilgrims, trudging to and from the great abbeys, which is still a popular walk today.

A third path ran south-east from Edinburgh following the line of the present A62. First crossing the fertile lands of Midlothian, heading to Newbattle Abbey near Dalkeith, it then rose over the bare and windswept hills of the Lammermuirs to

The Font Stone, about 2 miles from the village of Nine
Mile Burn. Perhaps once used for baptisms, it is now
believed to be lucky to throw coins into the basin
hollowed out in the stone

Soutra Summit, 363m high. A hospice here
gave food and shelter to travellers who
struggled, particularly in winter weather,
over roads made treacherous by wind and ice.

Continuing south-east, the route follows
the Leader Water to its confluence with the
Tweed and onwards to the great abbeys of
Selkirk, Kelso, Dryburgh, Jedburgh and, most
particularly, Melrose, so beloved of Sir Walter
Scott.

MELROSE ABBEY

The Pilgrimage of the Black Douglas

D avid I, the sixth son of Malcolm III and Queen Margaret, was King of Scotland from 1124–53. He is now mostly remembered for the many churches which he built. Most famous among them are the great border abbeys of Melrose and Jedburgh. So much money did he spend that his descendant, James I, was to call him 'A sair sanct to the croun' (a sore saint to the crown).

Melrose, the most beautiful of all his creations, is in Roxburghshire. It was founded by King David in 1136, 12 years into his reign. The Abbey stands just south of the great border river of the Tweed; St Cuthbert's monastery of Old Melrose being about two miles upstream. The chapel at Old Melrose – the name means 'bare promontory' – remained a place of pilgrimage until at least 1437 when pilgrims are known to have visited the chapel on 20 March, the feast day of St Cuthbert (who was later to become the Bishop of Lindisfarne).[1]

When the Abbey, which took ten years to complete, was built, King David invited the Cistercian monks of Rievaulx, in Northumberland, to inhabit it. One of the first abbots – possibly the very first – was David's own step-son, Waltheof, who was installed in 1148 and afterwards became a saint. It may have been in his time that, during a famine, no

less than 4,000 starving people are claimed to
have been fed by the monks of the monastery
for the whole of three months. A later bishop,
in 1175, was Jocelin, afterwards famous as
Bishop of Glasgow; Abbot Robert (1268) was
a former Chancellor of Scotland; while Abbot
Andrew (1449) went on to become Lord High
Treasurer.[2]

It was King Robert I, Robert the Bruce,
King of Scotland from 1306–29, who really
put Melrose on the map. In January 1326, he
granted the abbey £100 per annum to provide
each monk with the 'King's Dish' every day.
To pay for this indulgence, Melrose was to
receive the annual sum of £100 from the
'fermes or new custom' (customs tax) of
Berwick and from the custom tax on goods
imported and exported from Edinburgh and
Haddington. In return, the monks had to
promise to feed and clothe 15 of the poor on
Martinmas Day.

In addition to this, in March of the same
year (1326) the king gave instructions for the
renovation of the abbey. This was to be
funded by all his feudal revenue from the
whole county of Roxburgh until this should
amount to £2,000.[3] In a letter, the king
informed the abbot and his brethren that he
had appointed Lord James Douglas ('the
Black Douglas'), as superauditor of receipts
and expenses. The king explained how
Douglas, acting on royal instructions, would
enforce payment. Thus, both Tweedale and
the Lothians were charged with the

rebuilding of Melrose Abbey, together with the temporary support of the convent which had been established. Robert the Bruce had reason to be grateful to the convent: when Edward II of England had attacked it in 1322, the inmates had killed four of Edward's men.

By this time Robert the Bruce must have been afflicted by the first signs of the illness – commonly thought to have been leprosy – which, at that time, was such a scourge throughout most of the inhabited world. Knowing he was dying, the king gave instructions from the hall-house that he had built near his stronghold of Dumbarton Castle, on the estuary of the Clyde. From here he issued two documents, both dated 11 May 1329.[4] One was a Letter Patent of Protection of Melrose; the other contained commands to his sons and heirs to continue making payments to the abbey with the reminder that his heart was to be buried there.

Less than a month later, on 7 June, Robert the Bruce, who had won freedom for Scotland, was dead, aged only 55. He had planned to make a crusade to Jerusalem to visit the Holy Sepulchre, the tomb in which Christ was laid after the Crucifixion. However, as his health failed, he had decreed that his heart instead be taken 'to be born in battle against Saracens' by a crusading knight. Accordingly, 'the Black Douglas', the man who had been Bruce's greatest supporter throughout his many campaigns, took up the charge.

In September 1329, Edward III of England issued letters of protection on behalf of Lord Douglas, together with a commendation to King Alfonso XI of Castile. Sailing early in the following year, Douglas landed first in Flanders before going onwards to Coruña to fight the Moorish King of Granada. In August, while besieging the town of Teba de Ardules, Douglas, who is thought to have ridden too far ahead of his men, was ambushed. Surrounded and knowing he could not survive, he hurled Bruce's heart in its silver casket into the midst of his enemies before he died at their hands.

Somehow the casket was retrieved and returned to Scotland to be buried, as Bruce had wished, in the Chapter House of Melrose Abbey. The heart of the hero king, together with the bones of St Waltheof (former abbot of Melrose Abbey), attracted so many pilgrims that, eventually, access to the Chapter House had to be banned. A pilgrim's badge, depicting a rose encircled within a mason's mel, significant of Melrose, is now in the National Museum of Scotland.

In 1385 the English soldiers of Richard II set fire to the abbey. Melrose then became a busy place as reconstruction of the abbey continued for over more than 150 years.

Finally, the abbey, cruciform in shape, built in the English perpendicular decorated and flamboyant styles, was complete. It was 250 feet long and was distinguished by what has been described as the 'fairy-like lightness

The Pilgrim's Badge of Melrose, showing
the rose within the mason's mel
(courtesy of the Trustees of the National
Museums of Scotland)

of its carvings and window-tracery finished
with exquisite care.'[5] The great traceried-
window in the south transept and the
perpendicular windows of the east presbytery
remain complete. Sir Walter Scott, inspired by
their beauty, wrote in his poem, the 'Lay of
the Last Minstrell':

> *The moon on the east oriel shone*
> *Through tender shafts of stately stone.*
> *By foliaged tracery combined.*
> *Thou wouldst have thought some fairy's*
> *   hand*
> *Twixt poplars straight the osier wand,*
> *In many a freakish knot had twined.*
> *Then framed a spell when the work was*
> *   done*
> *And changed the willow wreaths to stone.*

The abbey was again damaged in 1544, when, during the war known as the 'Rough Wooing', the troops of Henry VIII burned Melrose and looted the surrounding area. Nonetheless, it was again restored. This was largely due to the richness of its endowment in both land and possessions, which, by the early 1500s, was reckoned to provide an annual revenue worth at least £100,000 in today's money – an enormous sum at the time. Today the towering ruins of the abbey, built of sandstone which glows pink in the setting sun, symbolise its former magnificence. Although laid out on the lines of the original monastery, the structure is nearly entirely that of the Gothic abbey which replaced it during the 15th century.[6]

By the middle of the next century the brotherhood of the abbey, originally 200 strong, had been reduced to about 150. Following the Reformation in 1560, however, the monks were so ruthlessly driven out that only 11 received pensions at the dissolution of the monastery.[7]

Devastation then followed when the abbey was wrecked by fanatical Presbyterians in 1569. Carvings, thought to be idolatrous, were cast down and destroyed while stones were purloined to be used for new houses in the town.

Fortunately, the abbey was later acquired by the Buccleuch family who eventually gave it to the nation so that it is now in the care of Historic Scotland.

In 1996, a team of expert archaeologists were excavating the site and found a lead container below the floor of the Chapter House. Under laboratory conditions a small hole was drilled into the casket so that the interior could be investigated with a fibre-optic cable. The large casket having been carefully opened, a smaller lead container was found within. Attached to it was an engraved copper plaque which read:

> *The enclosed leaden casket, containing*
> *a heart, was found beneath the*
> *Chapter House Floor, March 1921,*
> *by His Majesty's Office of Works.*

Richard Wellander, one of the investigating team from Historic Scotland, said that although it was not possible to prove absolutely that it is Bruce's heart, it was 'reasonable to assume that it is'. There are no records of anyone else's heart being buried at Melrose.

The casket containing the heart was buried again at Melrose Abbey on 22 June 1998. Two days later, on the anniversary of Bruce's great victory at the Battle of Bannockburn in 1314, the late Donald Dewar, then Scottish Secretary of State, unveiled a plinth over the place in the abbey grounds where the heart is now buried.

Thus, 669 years after his death, the heart of the king who freed Scotland was finally laid to rest.

DUNFERMLINE ABBEY

St Margaret's Priory or King David's Abbey

St Margaret, who was born in Hungary, was the granddaughter of Edward Ironside. Following the death of Edward the Confessor, the English Parliament asked her father, known as Edward the Exile, to become king. He reached England but died almost on arrival.

Following the Norman Conquest of England in 1066, his son, Edgar Atheling, had to flee the country. He sailed for the Continent, but his ship was driven off course in a fierce storm and he came ashore with his family in a Fife harbour, now called St Margaret's Hope. When Malcolm III, King of Scots, was told of their arrival, he came to welcome them and fell in love with Atheling's sister, the beautiful Princess Margaret. They married in the church of Dunfermline, which Malcolm himself had built in 1070.

The Queen, together with her chaplain Turgot,[8] (who had been sent to Scotland by Lanfranc, Archbishop of Canterbury), worked ceaselessly to bring the Celtic churches of the Culdees under the auspices of Rome. In 1072, she enlarged her husband's church and founded a Benedictine priory at Dunfermline. Here it was that she laid down the rules which brought the Culdee settlements into the Continental system of monasticism.

Dunfermline Abbey, where pilgrims once
worshipped at St Margaret's Shrine

Margaret never learned Gaelic but her
husband, the king, translated her words so
that all those within the church could
understand their meaning.

In her own lifetime, she encouraged
pilgrims to visit Dunfermline and the nearby
town of St Andrews, seat of the Scottish
primacy. Queensferry was described in Latin
as *Passagium Sancte Margarete Regine* (passage
of St Margaret the Queen) and the burgh seal
of South Queensferry shows St Margaret in a
boat about to land. In her right hand she

holds a sceptre; in her left, a book. The ferry service, which she subsidised to take pilgrims across the Forth, ended only when the Forth Road Bridge was opened in 1964.

St Leonard's Hospital in Dunfermline is traditionally thought to have been founded by St Margaret. The Rev. Peter Chalmers, writing in 1844, affirmed that 'the hospital was situated a little to the south of the Hospital [Spittal] Bridge, at the lower end of the town, on the east side of the road leading to Queensferry . . . the hospital was endowed for the support of eight widows, each of whom, in addition to certain grants, had a small garden and a room within the building.'[9]

On 16 November 1093, the Queen, by then lying mortally ill in Edinburgh Castle, learned of the death of her husband and her eldest son at Alnwick. The shock apparently killed her. Edinburgh Castle was being besieged by her brother-in-law, Donald Bane, who subsequently became King of Scotland from 1094–7, yet somehow her body was smuggled out and taken to Dunfermline. There she was buried before the altar of the church which she had built.

Queen Margaret's second son, King Edgar, who died in 1106, was also buried in Dunfermline. Her third son, Alexander I, brought his father's body from Tynemouth to lie beside that of his mother. Then, when he himself died, in 1124, he was also interred within his mother's church.

North Queensferry. The landing place of the ferry, on
the north shore of the Forth, which was founded by St Margaret
to take pilgrims across the river

David I, Queen Margaret's sixth son,
made her priory into an abbey in 1128. The
nave of the great Romanesque church, its
massive sculptured pillars inspired by those
of Durham Cathedral, still stands within the
cathedral which was rebuilt in 1818.

Queen Margaret was canonised in 1250. In
the same year, Alexander III transferred the
body of his great-great-great-grandmother
from the stone tomb where she had lain for
143 years and placed her remains within a
silver shrine set with gold and precious
stones. The shrine, which stood beside
St Margaret's altar, was much visited by
pilgrims until the Reformation when the
jewels and precious metals were stolen or
destroyed.

St Margaret's head, with its auburn hair, eventually ended up in the Scots College at Douay, but it vanished during the Revolution. Other relics of both the queen and her husband, Malcolm, were taken to Spain and secreted in two urns within the walls of the Escorial, the royal palace near Madrid.[10]

King Robert the Bruce, who died in 1329, was buried before the high altar of Dunfermline Abbey. His body, found in a stone tomb when the abbey was being re-built in 1818, was afterwards returned to the place where it had lain for nearly 500 years.

Bruce was a national hero. Nonetheless, it is St Margaret, the Saxon princess who came as a refugee to Scotland, whose name has been so closely associated with Dunfermline for over 1,000 years.

St Andrews Cathedral
Dedicated to Scotland's Patron Saint

On the North Sea coast, midway between the Firths of Forth and Tay, St Andrews was originally the Pictish settlement of Kilrymont. The fact that the Gaelic word *cill* means 'cell' or 'chapel' indicates a Christian settlement.

The legend of St Andrews tells how St Andrew, brother of St Peter, was crucified at Patros. His bones were later taken to

Constantinople and enshrined.

A later story dates from the time of the Pictish King Ungus, or Hungus (Angus), who reigned from 731 to 761. It relates how the king 'rising with a great army against the British nations . . . came at last to the plain of the Merse', the fertile lowland area of S.E. Scotland, north of the Tweed. Here he wintered.

St Andrew and the Scottish Saltire

'Then came nearly the whole of the natives of the island and surrounded him . . . but next day, when the king was walking with his seven most intimate companions, a divine light surrounded them, and, falling on their faces, they heard a voice from heaven saying, "Ungus, Ungus, hearken unto me, the apostle of Christ called Andrew, who am sent to defend and protect you. Behold the sign of the cross in the air; let it advance against your enemies. You must however offer up the tenth part of your inheritance as an oblation to God omnipotent, and in honour of St Andrew."

'On the third day King Ungus divided his army into 12 troops, each preceded by the sign of the cross, and they were victorious.'[11] King Angus then returned to his camp near Jarrow firmly resolved to uphold his promise to St Andrew the apostle.

A later version of the legend tells how 'some days after this victory, the angel of God appears to the blessed bishop Regulus' (to

163

whom some of the bones and a tooth of
St Andrew had been entrusted in
Constantinople) and warns him to sail to the
north . . . 'and wherever his vessel should be
wrecked, there to erect a church in honour of
St Andrew'. The bishop follows these
instructions and eventually arrives 'at a place
called Muckros, but now Kylrimont.'[12]

However, it is generally believed that
what actually happened was that monks of
the Columban clergy, expelled by the
Northumbrians from Hexham, found a new
home in Scotland.

When Bede wrote in 731, Bishop Acca was
still in Hexham but, according to Simeon of
Durham, Acca was forced to leave the
following year. The historian W.F. Skene says,
'it is certainly a remarkable coincidence that
Acca, the venerator of St Andrew and the
importer of relics into Hexham, should have
fled in 732, that a report should have sprung
up that he had founded a See amongst the
Picts; and that St Andrews should have been
actually founded by a Pictish king between
the years 736 and 761, and part of the relics of
St Andrew brought to it at that time.'[13]

A monastery at St Andrews is mentioned
in the Irish annals as early as 747 and it is
known that the Culdee monks had their own
Church of the Blessed Mary of the Rock,
which stood between the precinct wall of the
cathedral and the sea, the foundations of
which can still be seen. The nave of this is
believed to date from as early as the 9th

century (transepts and a choir were added later) and because the relics of St Andrew are thought to have been kept there, this was the place to which the first pilgrims were drawn.

It is notable that the patron saint of Scotland never actually set foot on Scottish soil while alive. The relics of St Andrew were allegedly brought to Scotland by St Rule, also known as St Regulus.

The Church of St Rule, attributed to the latter part of the 11th century, was probably part of the episcopate of Fothad II, last of the Celtic bishops (c.1059–93). Standing just south-east of the Cathedral, it has been described as 'the finest of the small family of Square Tower churches, and probably a reliquary church.' Consisting originally of a square tower and a choir, a nave and a chancel were added in the early 12th century by Bishop Robert of St Andrews, the Norman prior, who brought with him Augustinian canons from Scone.

St Andrew's relics were guarded high within the tower. Consisting of nothing but a tooth and a few pieces of bone, they were kept in a small but splendid casket, known as the Morbrac, or Great Reliquary, which was light enough to be carried in procession.

Not so was the sarcophagus which was also lodged within the tower. Large enough to hold a crouched figure, it may have been the sepulchre of St Rule himself. Hacked to pieces during the Reformation (when the Reliquary was also probably destroyed), parts of it were found in 1883 when a grave was dug beside the church. The surviving front panel – one of the greatest examples of Dark Age art – shows David rending the lion's jaws. His robes, hunting knife and the lion's curled mane are suggestive of Eastern design, although the whole depicts a Pictish hunting scene. A cleverly constructed restoration of the tomb stands within the museum of St Andrew's Cathedral today.[14]

These were the relics which drew pilgrims in their thousands to St Andrews. The first recorded is Aed, a prince of Ireland, who died 'in pilgrimage' at St Andrews in 965. A century later, so many people came that Queen Margaret, wife of Malcolm III, established the ferry which took them across the Forth, free of charge, from North to South Queensferry: places which still acknowledge their gratitude in their names.

Pilgrims coming from the north-west – from Perth and the great Augustinian abbey of Scone – were ferried across the River Tay

The surviving side of the St Andrews Sarcophagus
(Crown Copyright reproduced courtesy of Historic Scotland)

just below its confluence with the Earn. From there, their way can still be followed to Gallows Hill and on to the abbey of Lindores, where the monks restored them with food and home-brewed ale from their own farm.

From Lindores, they continued to the River Eden, where once again they had to cross by a ferry or else wade across a ford. This was dangerous, the river being tidal. The tragic drowning of 20 important churchmen probably prompted Bishop Wardlaw to build a bridge across the Eden, just to the west of St Andrews, in 1419.[15]

At that time, travelling was very hazardous in every way. Not only were the roads atrocious, little more than tracks at best, but thieves and beggars lurked along the known pilgrim routes. So greatly were the pilgrims preyed upon that, by the beginning of the 11th century, hostels where they could sleep in safety, and staging posts, where they gathered before proceeding on their way, were already being built. It was safer to travel as part of a group than to journey alone.

In 1144, Robert, the former prior of Scone, now Bishop of St Andrews, established the bishopric and an Augustinian cathedral-chapter (a meeting place for the canons of the cathedral), in the town which had become the ecclesiastical centre of Scotland. St Andrews was soon to become the wealthiest of all the religious houses in the land.

The Cathedral of St Andrews, linked to the Church of St Rule by a narrow choir, was founded in 1162. At 355 feet long (108m), it was the second largest church in Britain, surpassed only by Norwich Cathedral. Reputed to hold the relics of the apostle, it became a place of veneration to which Edward I made an offering in March 1304. Later, King Robert the Bruce gave 100 marks yearly to the cathedral, in gratitude to St Andrew, who he believed had aided his victory at Bannockburn in 1314.

The foundation charter of St Leonard's College, dated 1512, records that 'from divers lands, far and near, divers pilgrims did set forth to the Church of St Andrew because of the wonders for which the relics of the blessed apostle became famous, and in the zeal of their devotion thronged thither from day to day; and for the reception of these pilgrims the prior and convent of our church aforesaid did out of their piety build an hospital of St Andrews.'[16]

In 1273 much of the cathedral had to be rebuilt following a violent storm. Later destruction during the Reformation left just walls standing open to the battering of wind and rain. Today, only the east front, with its magnificent twin towers, remains to testify to the glory of a bygone age.

Parts of the adjoining Augustinian priory which survive include the ancient warming house which is now the museum. Within it are fragments of the grave-slabs of people of the Culdee settlement, which is known to have existed here at least 1,400 years ago.

DUNBLANE CATHEDRAL
Rare and Beautiful Gothic Survivor

An early Celtic foundation, probably a church of the Culdees, is thought to have stood on the site of the cathedral before the bishopric was founded *c*.1150. The square tower, originally four storeys high (to which another two were added in the 16th century), is believed to have been built as early as *c*.1090–1110.

The shrine of Columba – not the saint of Iona but the companion of the Irish St Blane, to whom the church was dedicated – was housed within the tower (*see page 100*). It became so greatly venerated by pilgrims that, in the 13th century, rather than demolishing the tower to build the new cathedral, the cathedral was built beside it.

The nave of Dunblane, of exceptional artistry, was the inspiration of Bishop Clement, a most remarkable man. Born in Scotland, he was educated in Paris where he became a friar of the Dominican order. Renowned for the power of his preaching, he returned to his homeland to found a number of Dominican houses. Then, in 1233, he was made Bishop of Dunblane.

Horrified by the state of his church, he complained to the Pope that the diocese had no money, that there was no cathedral chapter, that he himself was without a house, and that there was only one chaplain who officiated in a church without a roof!

Pope Gregory IX, much perturbed by this report, ordered the bishops of Glasgow and Dunkeld to investigate the matter and building began forthwith.

The result was a cathedral which, by the Middle Ages, had grown to be a famous monastic establishment. Bishop Clement died in 1258, but work was carried on sporadically by his successors for nearly 300 years. It was finally finished in the time of Bishop James Chisholm, who resigned the See in 1527.[17]

The nave of the cathedral is 129 feet in length and the choir is 81 feet. Carved stalls within the church, some of them canopied, are believed to date from the early 1500s – Bishop Chisholm's time. The effect that it has on the beholder is thus described:

> This cathedral is one of our noblest
> structures, and situated as it is on the
> high east bank of the Allan, which
> here swells out into a broad expanse,
> the views of the edifice, as seen from
> the south-west, with its lofty front and
> ancient tower rising above the wooded
> bank of the stream, is particularly
> charming.[18]

John Ruskin wrote of the Cathedral of St Blane, 'I know not anything so perfect in its simplicity and so beautiful in all the Gothic.' Incidentally, the cathedral was also dedicated to the Spanish saint, St Lawrence. As deacon of the Church of Rome, he was burnt alive over a grid-iron for refusing to relinquish the treasures of the Church to the pagan prefect of the city in AD258.

Following the Reformation, Dunblane Cathedral was so much neglected that only the choir remained in its original form. Fortunately, the roof of the nave and much of the interior were restored to their former beauty by Sir Robert Rowan Anderson and Sir Robert Lorimer in 1912–14.

The cathedral is one of the most impressive examples of medieval architecture in Scotland. From the time of its foundation it has remained the nucleus of the little town. People have gathered here to pray for deliverance from danger, from illness such as the plague, and to seek solace when tragedy occurred. Brass plaques on the floor of the choir mark the graves of Margaret Drummond, mistress of King James IV of Scotland, and her sisters who, when Margaret was thought to be a threat to the king's marriage with Margaret Tudor in 1503, were killed by poison in the nearby Castle of Inchaffray.

In modern times, the ancient cathedral again became a place of sanctuary for the hundreds of people who were plunged into shock and sorrow by the wanton murder of children and their teacher in Dunblane Primary School.

THE GREAT ABBEY OF SCONE
Ancient Seat of the Kings of Scotland

S t Boniface, or Alba, as he is also called, was an Irish Pict who was probably educated at Bangor or at one of the great daughter-houses of that Pictish educational centre. He is known to have attended the Irish Synod, when Adomnan was present, in 697. He is claimed to have become a devotee of Rome and the cult of St Peter, which was in vogue at that time.

The date of his arrival in Scotland is not recorded but it is said that he came as an architect-priest in answer to a summons from the Pictish King Nectan II, who wanted to build churches in his realm. No doubt, Boniface intended that they should be dedicated to his patron saint.[19]

From Northumbria, he sailed up the east coast of Scotland into the estuary of the Tay. Then he navigated his boat up the river, past Perth, to Scone. Welcomed by King Nectan, St Boniface baptized him, together with many of his court, into the Roman faith. According to Dr Skene, 'the king then dedicated the place of his baptism to the Holy Trinity, and gave it to Bonifacius and his bishops'.

Dr Skene goes on to suggest that the famous 'Coronation Stone', taken by Edward I of England to Westminster Abbey and now in Edinburgh Castle, may have been the stone altar on which Boniface first celebrated the Eucharist (or Lord's Supper) after he had brought over the King of the Picts and his people from the usages of the independent Columban Church and under the direction of Rome.[20]

Scone was an ancient seat of the kings of Scotland. The original church is said to have been occupied by the Culdees, the brotherhood of the old Celtic Church which was independent of Rome. In 1114, Alexander I, second of the sons of Queen Margaret and King Malcolm III, either enlarged or rebuilt what was probably just a small chapel into a priory for Augustinian monks. In this work he was assisted by Prior Adelwald of Nostell who is said to have sent canons from his own priory to Scone.

The priory became an abbey on 5 December 1164. A charter of Malcolm IV, in the same year, states that, after the church of Scone had been destroyed by fire, the king had constituted an abbot in it 'for the stability and advancement of that church'.

However, the abbey was pillaged and burnt again by the army of Edward I in 1298, this being about the time when the Stone of Destiny, together with other treasures of Scotland, was carried off to Westminster. The abbey must then have been substantially rebuilt for the abbot was mitred on 12 September 1395.[21]

Further devastation followed in 1559 when fanatical Reformers, inflamed by John Knox's impassioned speech at Perth, destroyed all they could find. The monastery, houses and church are reported in a charter, dated 26 August 1559, 'to be now burned to the ground'.

Scone then belonged to the Earl of Gowrie until, following 'the Gowrie Conspiracy' to kidnap James VI & I, his lands were forfeited to the crown. Afterwards, they were granted to Sir David Murray, ancestor of the Earl of Mansfield.[22]

Charles II was the last king of Scotland (and later of England) to be crowned at Scone in 1651.

During the 17th century, a house was built on the site of the now ruined abbey. Parts of this building are said to be incorporated into Scone Palace, which was designed by William Atkinson in 1802. The house, now open to the public, is the home of the Earl of Mansfield.

Visitors admiring its magnificence will find it hard to visualize the simple little church of the Early Christian Picts that once stood on this site. Yet we are told that it was here that St Boniface, no doubt stiff after his long voyage, was welcomed by the Pictish King Nectan II whom he had come to baptize.

Boniface left Scone to travel to Angus and then to Aberdeenshire in his great endeavour to bring the Celtic church under the rules of Rome. The churches he built were, almost without exception, dedicated to St Peter. Also, he is credited with the foundation of the ecclesiastical centre of Peterhead.

Further north in Thurso, where he built a

church, the town coat of arms shows the saint with the keys of heaven clutched in his left hand. In the Orkneys, and even in Lewis, churches and places bearing the name of St Peter are believed to relate to St Boniface.

Finally, at the age of 80, he retired to Rosemarkie, in the Black Isle, where, following his death, he was buried in the church he had renamed St Peter's.[23]

DUNKELD CATHEDRAL
Jewel of Picturesque Perthshire

In 806, St Columba's Abbey in Iona was destroyed by the Vikings, its monks brutally murdered on the shore. The abbey was rebuilt, but was so constantly pillaged by Norsemen, sweeping down from Orkney in their long boats, that it ceased to be the focus of the Columban houses in Scotland.

Many of the treasures of Iona, including the *Book of Kells*, were taken to Ireland for safety, but others went to the monastic settlement by the River Tay at Dunkeld, which replaced Iona in importance.[24]

Around 815, a Columban monastery had been founded at Dunkeld by Constantine, King of the Picts. Two Pictish grave slabs lie within the choir. Some 46 years later, in 851, Kenneth

The decorated capital 'S' in the Book of Kells

MacAlpine, who, seven years earlier had united the Scots and Pictish thrones, either completed the existing building or founded another, again dedicated to St Columba.

Dunkeld was a church of the Culdees until Queen Margaret's time. Then in 1107, her son, Alexander I, raised the status of the abbey of Dunkeld into that of a cathedral and appointed the abbot, Cormac, as the first bishop of an enormous See which stretched as far as Argyll.[25]

From there, pilgrims trudged across the desolate Rannoch Moor. Having sailed up Loch Rannoch, they headed for the west end of Loch Tummel. Then, going south through the Sma' Glen, they reached the great River Tay to follow it down to Dunkeld.

Another pilgrim route from Argyll began at Auch (Auchinchisallan), a farm which lies below and to the east of the A82, about four miles north of Tyndrum. The sheer heights of Beinn Dorain rise above it to the north and those of Ben Callum to the south. Between the two mountains, a track runs up and over the watershed to the head of Loch Lyon.

From there, the ancient route continues down the twisting turns of Glen Lyon – the longest glen in Scotland – to where, at the foot of its strath, the now smooth flowing river joins the Tay.

From the north, pilgrims came down Glen Garry to follow the River Tummel which also runs into the Tay. Those coming from the east either rode or walked up the north bank of this river, and pilgrims from the south would have been ferried across it from Inver. This continued to be the main crossing place until 1809 when Telfer built his famous bridge downstream.

The choir of the cathedral, when restored in the early 1900s, did show traces of 13th-century work. The main structure, however, does date from about 100 years later. The building of the nave is known to have begun in the time of Bishop Robert de Cardeney, in 1406, and to have been been finished by Bishop Lauder over 40 years afterwards.

During the 31 years of Lauder's episcopate, from 1450 to 1481, the 24 miracles of St Columba were painted above the high altar beneath two statues of the saint. This proved a magnet to the pilgrims who converged in even greater numbers upon the cathedral town. An added attraction was the tomb of Alexander Stewart, the 'Wolf of Badenoch'. Far from being a saint, he was the man who burnt Elgin Cathedral in 1390 after a quarrel with the bishop (*see page 179*). Nonetheless, his effigy, clad in 14th-century armour, still lies resplendent in the choir.

Even more miraculous were the happenings in the time of Lauder's successor, Bishop George Brown. In 1500, plague struck the people of Caputh, tenants of the cathedral sited only five miles away. Bishop Brown sent them some water in which the bones of the saint had been dipped. Those who drank the water, recovered; those who did not, died.

Not everyone, however, was convinced of the validity of the cure; before he perished, one man reputedly remarked, 'For what does the bishop send us water to drink? I could wish he had sent us some of his best ale!'

During the Reformation of 1560, or shortly afterwards, the roof of the cathedral was taken off and the walls left open to the skies. It was further damaged in 1689 when the army of the Presbyterian government, gallantly defending the town against the Royalists, exchanged fire with their enemies from within the shelter of the walls.

The ruined choir of the cathedral, now restored, is the modern-day Parish Church of Dunkeld.

ELGIN CATHEDRAL

The Lantern of the North

Elgin Cathedral towers stark against the sky, imperious and dominant as though defiant of decay. It seems oblivious of progress after 900 years. First built as a smaller church in the 12th century, it was enlarged after a fire to become the second greatest in Scotland – 280 feet long, surpassed only by St Andrews. Positioned just outside the burgh of Elgin, it was adjoined by its own walled township, the chanonry, where the priests dwelt.

Generously endowed by Alexander II, the church was consecrated as the Cathedral of Moray in 1224.[26]

In 1390, the Bishop of Moray, Bishop Bur, quarrelled ferociously with Alexander Stewart, Earl of Buchan ('Wolf of Badenoch'), a renegade brother of King Robert III. The reasons for this feud were twofold. Firstly, the Earl of Buchan had sworn to be protector and defender of the bishop on payment of a sum of money, which amounted to blackmail. The bishop had reneged on this arrangement and instead had promised to pay a pension to Thomas Dunbar, Sheriff of Inverness and son of the Earl of Moray. Secondly, the bishop, having accused the Earl of Buchan of mistreating his wife and flaunting his mistresses, received permission from the Pope to excommunicate him. Furious, the Wolf of Badenoch was quick to take revenge. On 17 June 1390, Elgin Cathedral went up in flames.

Bishop Bur was left lamenting over the cinders that had once been 'the ornament of the realm, the glory of the kingdom, the delight of foreigners and stranger guests'.[27]

The restoration which followed lasted for 200 years. The west front, comprising a portal between two towers, with its magnificent traceried window and double-doored portal screen, remains as proof of the skill of the masons of those days. The octagonal Chapter House with its elaborate ceiling was redecorated c.1500. Traces of gold paint can still be seen on the vaulting.

Sadly, however, the cathedral had but a brief return to glory. The Reformation of 1560, which caused so much desecration to Scottish churches, did not spare the wonderful building called the 'Lantern of the North'. The bishops moved to the parish church of St Giles, in Elgin, leaving the cathedral to the mercy of the vandals who quickly removed the lead flashings and the bells. In 1637, the roof blew off in a gale whereupon the rood-screen and other fittings were purloined for firewood. The stone walls, left open to the elements, began to disintegrate and finally, in 1711, the central tower collapsed, taking with it most of the nave.

The great church then lay deserted. Only the Chapter House was used as a meeting room by Elgin tradesmen. Thus things remained until, in 1807, John Shanks, a 'douthy cobbler' was made keeper of the cathedral. Single handed, he struggled on to clear the rubble, heaving stones from the collapsed piles of masonry. Then at last, inspired by his efforts, the burgh authorities produced a report which detailed the work needed to stabilize the ruin and improve its surrounds. This resulted in a joint project by the Office of Works and the Burgh Council.

Today, one can only marvel at the artistry of the great east gable with its many windows which include a lancet and a rose. Much of the choir and the presbytery remain. The aisles and chapels on either side of the choir have been altered, but the vaults have survived since 1270. Most importantly, the octagonal Chapter House, rebuilt 500 years ago, and re-roofed during 1987–9 survives largely unchanged. The 'Lantern of the North' is, as it was when it was first built, a great landmark of Moray, visible from miles around and is now in the care of Historic Scotland.[28]

PLUSCARDEN ABBEY

Hallowed Retreat

While Elgin Cathedral remains in ruined magnificence, nearby Pluscarden Abbey retains 'the atmosphere of quiet reflection and of work dedicated to the glory of God [which is] the same today as it was in the 13th century . . . under the skilful hands of the present-day brethren, Pluscarden is a living entity that is returning again to something approaching its former splendour after a long period of pillage and decay.'

Destruction began in 1390 when the savagery of Alexander Stewart, the 'Wolf of Badenoch', knew no bounds. Because it was under the authority of Bishop Bur, Pluscarden proved a prime target for his sworn enemy. Obsessed with his hatred of Bishop Bur, the Wolf attacked the Priory, leaving it largely in ruins, its walls blackened and roofless, standing open to the sky.

Pluscarden Priory was founded by Alexander II in 1230, four years before the consecration of Elgin Cathedral, so wantonly destroyed. The king, who had an eye for fine sites, chose to place it six miles (10km) from Elgin in a wide, sun-kissed valley beneath the shelter of Heldon Hill. Here, the monks of the original brotherhood of the Valliscaulian Order raised cattle and grew crops to sustain themselves as well as the poor, the sick and the travellers to whom they gave shelter and rest. The priory, dedicated to St Mary, St John and St Andrew, was one of the three Valliscaulian foundations in Scotland which were linked to the Priory of Val des Choux in Burgundy (*see page 96*). The others are Beauly, in Ross (west of Inverness) and Ardchattan on the shore of Loch Etive in Argyll.

Following the devastation of the 'Wolf of Badenoch' in 1390, Pluscarden Priory was partly restored. Records of rents of land, mills and fishing on the Spey being paid to Pluscarden show that the Priory was not entirely destitute, although the buildings needed much repair. The year 1454 also saw Pluscarden united to the nearby Benedictine Priory of Urqhuart. Urquhart Priory, like its mother-house Dunfermline Abbey, was a Benedictine foundation. Therefore 'ecclesiastically, this date marks the disappearance from Moray of the white habits of the Valliscaulians and their replacement by the black dress of the old Benedictines of Dunfermline and Urquhart.'

The Benedictines brought new life to the Priory. Robert Harrower, originally a monk of Dunfermline, was elected Prior of Pluscarden from 1487 to 1509. It was he who welcomed James IV to the Priory when the King, who probably stopped here on one of his many pilgrimages to Tain, gave 'drink-silver' to masons working on the Priory.

Alexander Dunbar, from a powerful local family, was prior from 1529 to 1560. His brother, James, was the baillie who administered the Barony of Pluscarden, as is proved by the rent books. The lands were

Ardchattan Priory. The house, to which additions were made in the 19th century, still contains the original refectory of the monks of the Valliscaulian Order, who were established there c.1230

Pluscarden Abbey, the only medieval monastery in Britain which is still inhabited by monks (courtesy of Father Giles Conacher)

extensive – from the Church of Dores on the Banks of Loch Ness, to farms round Fochabers in the east. The rents, as in other places, were paid largely in kind: roebuck, sheep, poultry and oats, etc. The tenant of the brewery, however, had to produce an annual sum of 26 shillings and 8 pence.

The Dunbars, perhaps thanks to their affluence, had enemies. On 1 January 1555, Prior Dunbar and his relations were attacked by a local family called Innes in Elgin Cathedral. Swords flashed in the candlelight as 'apostolic blows and knocks' echoed throughout the cloisters. The 'bloody Vespers' eventually ended in a court case.

Prior Dunbar added the Dunbar Vestry to the Priory. He died in September 1560, just a month after the Catholic religion was proscribed by law in Scotland. Forseeing the Reformation, he bequeathed the Church lands to his family (he had legitimate children).

Nevertheless, in 1561, Mary Queen of Scots, a Catholic, banished the Dunbars and installed William Cranston, a priest, as Prior. Lord Seton, her strong supporter in Moray, was made Steward of the lands. In 1565, following Cranston's death, the priory was given to Seton's son, Alexander, the Queen's godson, who became the commendator, or layman in charge of the priory.

In 1587, Seton signed a charter with Thomas Ross, 'last of the monks', before he sold Pluscarden to Kenneth MacKenzie of Kintail, a Privy Councillor of King James VI & I, in 1595.

After the Reformation, the buildings again became ruins. 'All is cold and silent, forlorn and melancholy desolation; everything pleasant and useful is vanished,' reported the author of *A Survey of the Province of Moray, Aberdeen*, in 1708. Various owners did little to improve their state until, in the late 19th century, the buildings were rescued by John, 3rd Marquis of Bute, who, having been converted to Catholicism, made their restoration almost a lifetime's work. Nearly half a century later, in 1943, his son, Lord Colum Crichton-Stuart, handed the priory over to the Benedictine community of Prinknash Abbey in the English county of Gloucestershire.[29]

The monks, who returned to live in Pluscarden in 1948, continued with the great work of rebuilding the priory. Pluscarden was raised to the status of an abbey in 1974 and as such it remains the only medieval monastery in the United Kingdom still occupied by a brotherhood, who number 30 in all. This community is led by Abbot Hugh Gilbert, while Father Giles oversees the day-to-day running of the abbey, which is a hallowed retreat for an increasing number of visitors (for whom there is no entrance fee).

Today, most travel to Pluscarden by car. Perhaps some of the early ones paddled their coracles up the Black Burn, otherwise they must have tramped along tracks, either from Elgin or over the hill from Kinloss. The very fact that a pilgrim road runs along the north of the Precint Wall proves, without any doubt, that this has been a place of pilgrimage ever since 1230, when, over seven centuries ago, Alexander II chose to found a priory in this sheltered, secluded place.

BEAULY PRIORY

Beloved by Mary Queen of Scots

S t Drostan, thought to have been a Briton and possibly the uncle of St Adrian, is believed to have founded the first church at Beauly. The *Wardlaw Manuscript* refers to it as 'St Dunstance Priory Church'.[30]

The ruins of the later priory, built upon the same site, stand at the east end of the town. Founded by Sir John Bisset of Lovat in 1230, during the reign of Alexander II, it was one of the three priories of the Valliscaulian Order which was first established in Val des Choux in Burgundy (*see page 96*). Given the Latin name *Bello Loco* because of the beauty of its site, 'it was planted in a situation admirably suited for the object of its institution, amidst a tract of rich alluvial soil, brought down by the river, which stretched between the hills and seashore on the great high road from Inverness to the North'.

Bisset, who had recently acquired the large possessions of the Aird, sited the new monastery just where the river, after wasting the speed acquired by its rush over the rocks of Kilmorack, spreads out into the Beauly Firth. Opposite the wooded hills of Balblair and open to the sunny south, the priory was set amid fields of 'the finest wheat and the most luxuriant grasses'.[31]

The English baron's lands were joined to those of the Frasers of Lovat by marriage and the priory was completed by 1272. Sir Simon Fraser of Lovat was buried in front of the altar in the chancel in 1287.

In 1430, his descendant, Sir Hugh Fraser of Lovat, complained to the Pope that the priory was so neglected that the buildings were falling into decay. Forthwith, a programme of restoration began. The finished layout comprised a cloister to the south, together with a south and east range of buildings, wherein dwelt the monks, while a range to the west was the prior's lodging.

Around 1510, the Priory became Cistercian. Some 30 years later it was hit by lightning. Repairs were then once more carried out, this time under the auspices of Prior Robert Reid, a man better known as the founder of Edinburgh University.

In 1560, following the prohibition of the Catholic faith by the Scottish Parliament, Reid became the priory's lay 'commendator', or non-clerical administrator. Standing beside 'the great high road to Inverness', the priory provided both rest and shelter to many travellers of all ranks of society. Prior Reid even received Mary Queen of Scots as his guest during her progress through the Highlands to Easter Ross.

The young Queen was entranced with her surroundings. *'Oui, c'est un beau lieu'* (Yes, it is a beautiful place), she reputedly said, her choice of words echoing its name.

Alas, following the Reformation, when so many church buildings were destroyed or damaged, the Priory at Beauly was not spared. The lead was stripped off the roof in 1582 before much of the building became a quarry for new houses in the town. Oliver Cromwell is said to have carried off stone as far as Inverness in 1652.

Today, only the north transept, rebuilt by Alexander Ross as a mausoleum for the MacKenzie family in 1901, remains to indicate the form of the original building. Taken over by the government in 1913, the Priory is now maintained by Historic Scotland.

SACRED TREASURES OF THE HEBRIDEAN ISLES & ORKNEY

From the early years of the 9th century, Vikings continued to sweep south from Orkney to raid the Scottish isles and the mainland. In Ireland, they set up trading posts in Dublin where they formed a settlement in 841. Once established, they spread to Limerick, Waterford and Wexford.

During the years of Viking occupation, the influence of the great religious houses in Ireland continued to expand. When Alcuin, the Northumbrian scholar, lived in Tours from 798–804, he worked with Irish scribes. In 975, the monastery of St Martin of Cologne was given over to the Irish and, during the 11th century, the monastery of St Martin of Maintz (also in Germany) had a majority of Irish monks. Irish and Germanic art bear many similarities from as early as the 7th century.

Pilgrimages from Ireland during the 11th century were made, either by way of Scotland, the Low Countries and Germany, or through France to Rome. Some travellers probably went all the way by sea to the south-west coast of France, journeying the rest of the way by river and land. So many took the largely overland route that some of the Continental monasteries were founded partly as resting places for Irish pilgrims on their way to the Holy Land.

At last, in 1014, the Irish defeated the Vikings at the battle of Clontarf, near Dublin. The victory was complete. After two centuries, the might of the invaders was crushed. Nonetheless, the Norsemen took home with them a quantity of Irish objects which greatly influenced Scandinavian art. The decorative style, based on elegant and flowing combinations of fantastically elongated animals, appears in the motifs on the Oseberg tomb in Norway. It most closely resembles the old Irish tradition.

Conversely, the Vikings themselves left emblems behind both in Ireland and later in Scotland. They include the strange animal heads whose whiskers and hair are made of large ribbons, usually interwoven. In addition, many medieval grave slabs depict the single-handed sword of Viking origin. These carvings prove that, even after the battle of Clontarf, Scandinavian fashions continued to be copied in Ireland. However, when Irish craftsmen imitated patterns, it was often their own art, subtly altered, which was actually the source of their inspiration.

190

While Scandinavian monuments derive from Irish examples, the reality may be a parallel phenomenon. The Lismore crosier and the Clonmacnois crosier depict thread-like animals which are contrived in an almost identical way to the carvings in the church at Urnes in Norway, the date of which is taken to be 1060–80.

Despite the destruction of the Norsemen, the church in Ireland survived. It was only just after the battle of Clontarf – at least before 1036 – that the Episcopal See was founded in Dublin. Subsequently, some 100 years later, c.1110, the Irish Church was brought under Rome.[1]

After this the journeys from Ireland to the Papal court increased. Travellers inspired by the great churches of Europe returned with acquired skills of architecture and classical design.

The influence of Carolingian art emerges in the initials, with animal terminals, interlacings and compositions of interlocked beasts, which appear in Romanesque illumination. Some of the best examples can be found in the pre-Reformation chapels in Knapdale and Kintyre.

Typical too are the foliage patterns, so much used in metalwork and manuscripts. The first great Limoges Bible, dating from the 11th century, shows animals alternating with acanthus leaves in the arches, while monsters fight on the pillars which support them. In addition, the voussoirs of the cathedral of

Angoulême have animals embroiled in conflict and bear an amazing similarity to the border interlacings of the Irish manuscripts. Thus, by the 11th century, this method of building up compositions on geometrical schemes seems to have been largely universal – a direct result of the pilgrimages.[2]

The perfection and increasing sophistication of the monumental sculpture and the illuminated manuscripts of this period also testify to the fact that Ireland, by this time, was revered throughout Europe as a centre of culture. Following the expulsion of the Vikings, it appeared that the zenith of creation had been achieved. Then – only 60 years after the battle of Clontarf – devastation returned.

This time invaders came from England. Norman knights, skilled in tactical warfare, over-ran the country. Men and horses, protected by steel armour, terrorised the local people. Once in predominance, the new conquerors divided the land into feudal estates and, in 1171, Henry II of England came to see his new territories. Ireland, held by Norman barons, was again a subject state.

Descended as they were from the Norsemen, the Normans, even while professing Christianity, proved to be as predatory as their ancestors. Like them, they robbed and vandalised the Irish churches. Nonetheless, they did introduce their own distinctive forms of architecture throughout the British Isles, which explains why English

Romanesque motifs did not begin to appear in Irish art before the 12th century.

Meanwhile, in Scotland and the Hebridean Isles the Vikings still held sway. It was only in 1156 that Somerled, son of the Thane of Argyll, defeated the Norse King Godred in a great sea-battle off Islay. Following this victory Somerled was acknowledged as ruler of all of the islands on the west coast south of the Treshnish Isles, which lie to the north-west of Mull.

Somerled divided his territory between three sons – Dugall, the progenitor of the Clan MacDougall; Reginald, ancestor of the MacDonalds; and Angus, whose inheritance descended to the MacRuaries when he died.

It was Reginald, Somerled's second son, who completed the great abbey at Saddell, allegedly founded by his father who is said to be buried there. Concurrently, in about 1202, Reginald began the massive task of rebuilding the abbey of Iona, by then reduced to ruins due to the Vikings' continual destruction over nearly 400 years. St Columba's buildings, and those of his successors, built of wood and thatched with turf, had been all too easily burnt. Reginald's walls were of stone, securely roofed with slate.

The Benedictine abbey of his construction is first mentioned in a bull of Pope Innocent III, dated 9 December 1203. It was addressed to Abbot Celestinus and his brethren, who took the new community and its property under the protection of the Holy See.[3]

Reginald is also credited with building the nunnery: his sister Beatrice being the first prioress. The *Book of Clanranald* (written in the 17th century) records the burials of Reginald, together with many of his male descendants (both of the senior MacDonald and of the Clanranald lines) in the burial-ground of Reilig Odhráin and within St Oran's Chapel. The chapel, standing towards the north end of Reilig Odhráin, is dedicated to St Oran, cousin and contemporary of St Columba. It is thought to have been built during the 12th century by Somerled, or his son Reginald, as a family mausoleum.

Some 200 years later, the monastery on Iona was again rebuilt when Abbott Dominic summoned the master-mason Donald ó Brolchán from Ireland to carry out a major programme of restoration.

The Irish mason arrived in Iona when many Scottish students, trained in Irish monasteries (notably in Armagh), were returning to their own country. Nonetheless, it was he who made Iona famous as a centre of monumental carving. He left his own memorial on a pillar of the south transept of Iona Abbey. The east nook-shaft capital of the south respond of the east crossing-arch bears a pattern of entwined plant-scrolls: an animal at the north-east angle grasps a plant-stem in its mouth, while the tail of one crouching opposite ends in an oak leaf with pendent acorns. The Lombardic inscription above, now damaged, but legible in 1844, read

'*Donaldus o [Brol/chan f] ecit hoc opus*, meaning 'Donald ó Brolchán made this work'.[4]

From this time onwards the work of the sculptors on Iona became increasingly renowned. The masons, working from pattern books, drew designs with the aid of compasses, before chiselling them on to blocks of the local stone. From the island they travelled elsewhere within the Lordship of the Isles – which then stretched from Kintyre and the island of Islay in the south to the Treshnish islands north of Mull – to instruct both clergy and laymen in their skills.

The Iona school led to the establishment of other schools of monumental sculpture. One was at Saddell Abbey on the east coast of Kintyre, and another was sited near Castle Suibhne (Castle Sween) on the west coast of the peninsula.

Farther north in Mid-Argyll a centre dubbed the 'Loch Awe School' was probably based near Kilmartin. The sculptors, whose work is thought to be inferior to those of the other schools, were itinerant workers who used local stone.

Sculptured grave slabs at Saddell Abbey. Some of the finest examples of effigies of Highland warriors and churchmen of medieval times

These West Highland schools of sculpture were sponsored by successive generations of the Lords of the Isles for nearly 300 years. This was a time that can truly be called a renaissance of Irish/Scottish art. In 1494, however, after internecine quarrelling and ruinous defeats, John, Lord of the Isles, resigned his territories to the young King James IV of Scotland. The great abbey of Iona, deprived of its sponsorship, then deteriorated so greatly that its status could not be maintained. Many of the monks were forced to find sanctuary in Ireland and elsewhere.

Fortunately, in this time of crisis, Mael-Sachlainn ó Cuinn, an Irish master-mason who had been working on Iona, found a refuge on the tidal island of Oronsay which lies to the south of Colonsay, just a short sail across the sea from Iona.

Oronsay had long been a place of sanctuary. People, whatever their crime, believed themselves safe when they had passed the now much weathered Sanctuary Rock embedded in the centre of the Strand.

The priory on Oronsay, a house of Augustinian monks, had been founded on the site of an earlier building, by John I, Lord of the Isles, circa 1325. Dedicated to St Columba, he had given it to the Church in gratitude for the Bill of Divorce which sanctioned his second marriage to the Princess Margaret, daughter of King Robert II.

The earliest buildings included the prior's house, most of the northern range and the

Oronsay Priory. Dedicated to St Columba by
John, Lord of the Isles, c.1325.

chapter house. The cloister and church were
added in the late 14th or early 15th century.
The office of prior had been held almost
continuously by the MacDuffies, a clan of
ancient descent, who had dwelt in Colonsay
and Oronsay since before recorded time.

In the early 1500s, following his flight
from Iona, Mael-Sechlainn ó Cuin was
employed by Colin MacDuffie, chief of his
clan, to build the cloister-arcade and to found
the Oronsay School of Monumental Sculpture
on the lines of the one he had been forced to
leave.

Ó Cuin is now mostly remembered by the
magnificent Oronsay Cross, which he erected
to the memory of Colin MacDuffie in the late
1400s. The inscription, in Lombardic letters, at
the foot of the east face of the stem of the
cross reads: *Hic est cr/ux Colini F/ilh Christi/ni
M(eic)duaci* – 'This is the cross of Colinus
(Malcolm, Gille-Coluim) son of Christinus
MacDuffie'.

Oronsay Cross. The wonderful work of the Irish mason who found sanctuary on Oronsay c.1500

Ó Cuinn, like ó Brolchán, carved his own epitaph. A most lovely and intricate foliate design, contrived within circles, decorates the west side of the cross. Below it another Lombardic inscription reads: *Maelseachl[ai]nd Saer/ [Ocuin] n Fecit ist [amc] Ruce [m]* – 'Mael-Sachlainn ó Cuinn, mason, made this cross'.[5] Thus is his name commemorated on one of the most beautiful carvings of the early 15th century, which, saved from destruction by the remoteness of Oronsay, remains as a legacy to the people of Scotland of today.

The Reformation, occurring some 60 years later, virtually annihilated the West Highland centres of art. On Iona, crosses, together with any religious icons considered idolatrous by Presbyterian zealots, were broken or hurled into the sea.

On Oronsay, Malcolm MacDuffie, successor to his father of the same name, assumed the title of Commendator, but the priory, unused by Presbyterian congregations, gradually fell into disrepair.

Fortunately, because of their weight and size, some of the greatest monuments proved to be indestructible. For this reason stones, which depict the designs which reached Ireland from East European and Mediterranean countries in early Christian times, survive to this day on the wind driven coasts of the Highlands and Hebridean Isles.

Oronsay Priory holds sculptured grave slabs of Highland warriors wearing armoured breastplates above quilted aketons and holding single-hand swords

ST CLEMENT'S CHURCH, RODEL
The Monument of the MacLeods of Harris

R enish Point, on the most southern tip of Harris, battered by wind and wave, is the last place on earth where one would expect to find carvings of such beauty that one can only stand and marvel at how they were achieved.

The chiefs of the MacLeods of Harris were buried on Iona – not so far from Harris as the crow flies. In 1528, however, Alexander MacLeod, the 8th chief, broke with tradition by bringing masons to Rodel (probably from Iona) to carve the incredibly designed wall-tomb in which he was buried in 1546.

Dean Munro, who came to Harris in 1549, wrote 'within the south pairt of this isle lyes ane monastery with ane stiepill, quhilk was foundit and biggit by McCloyd of harrey [Harris], callit Roodill'.[6]

St Clement was the patron saint of the MacLeods of Harris, and he is remembered in the 'Dunvegan Sea-hymn' which ends thus:

> *And we shall give the glory*
> *To the Trinity and Clement*
> *And the great clerk who lives in Rodel.*[7]

The rock of the Outer Hebrides is the oldest in the world. Much of it is exposed, but the red soil of Rodel (from the Norse word *rodil*, meaning red vale) gives good pasture. Good

land meant people settled here and a church,
possibly built first as a watch-tower, has
stood on Rodel from early times.

It is on record that, by the early 16th
century, the church at Rodel, to which that on
the nearby island of Pabbay was attached,
was the nucleus of the Christian settlements
of the Outer Isles. According to an old
tradition, treasures and artifacts from Rodel
were shipped to Rome for safety when the
Vikings over-ran the north-west coast of
Scotland.

In 1528, Alexander MacLeod of Harris,
known as Alasdair Crotach (hump backed)
because the muscles of his neck had been
broken by a sword or a battle-axe, began
rebuilding the church. The tower, thought to
be the oldest part, stands against a bluff of
rock which forms part of the structure up to
the first floor. A narrow internal staircase
connects the ground to the second floor, from
where fixed ladders reach a chamber beneath
the conical roof. Here lookouts strained their
eyes for enemy sails.

The stone is largely the local gneiss but a
string of coarse black schist, which crosses the
tower horizontally, gives a striking effect.
Panels on the west side include the effigy of a
bishop (supposedly St Clement who was
martyred by being thrown into the sea)
supported by a bull's head. There is also a
man in a kilt.

On the south wall a man and a woman in
crude positions are thought to be fertility

symbols, perhaps taken from an earlier building. A panel on the east wall depicts two fishermen in a boat, their net cleverly contrived from a piece of the black schist. A horse and a bull on the north wall are emblems of the MacLeods.

The shape of the church is cruciform. The nave and the choir, lying conjointly west to east, are crossed by transepts from north to south. The east window has a pointed arched head containing a wheel of six spokes.

In the south wall of the choir the effigy of Alasdair Crotach himself lies within his recessed tomb. Resplendent in plate armour with a bascinet (helmet) aventail and leg harness, he clasps a sheathed claymore. On his ankles above his abatons are straps to secure his spurs.

The sculptured voissoirs of the tomb, like the dressings of the church, are of yellowish freestone, probably brought from Carsaig on Mull where stone for the dressings of Iona Abbey was quarried in the 15th century. The overall design, reminiscent of a typanum like that on the west front of the great Abbey of Vézalay in western France, suggests European influence.

The voissoirs, nine in number, are arranged, four on each side, of the keystone which depicts the Holy Trinity. The others show the twelve apostles, grouped in pairs, with angels holding censors. Below is a triptych of the Virgin and Child with bishops on either side. A castle and a galley are emblems of the MacLeods. The ship is the model for the Aileach, sailed by a son of the present Clanranald from Ireland to Harris. St Michael and Satan are engrossed in the weighing of souls but it is the hunting scene, with Alasdair Crotach and his ghillies chasing stags, which seems to leap alive from the stone. This wealth of sculpture is without parallel on any Scottish wall-tomb.

The tomb of Alasdair's son, William, is also against the south wall. A third effigy in the South Transept is believed to be that of Ruairidh No Lann (Roderick of the Blades) a swordsman who, *c.*1739, rescued his wife from a ship on to which she had been lured to be sold as a slave in America.

Of the five grave-slabs in the North Transept two show 15th century warriors, the others being of later date. A disc headed cross on a window sill in the south wall of the nave depicts the Crucifixion and a stone bowl of great antiquity, probably a font, stands by the entrance to the tower.

In 1748 the church was restored by another Alexander MacLeod: an enterprising mariner who bought Harris from the trustees of his cousin, Norman MacLeod of Dunvegan. The work, interrupted by a fire, was finished in 1787.

In 1834, Alexander Norman (descended from the MacLeods) sold Harris to the Earl of Dunmore. Lady Dunmore, who established the tweed industry on a commercial basis, rebuilt St Clement's again in 1873.

In 1922 the then Earl of Dunmore entrusted the church to the Commissioners of his Majesty's Works and Public Buildings from which the Department of Historic Scotland has evolved.

The church was a place of sanctuary when land was held by the sword. A beggar's badge in lead, probably dating from the 17th century, was presented to the Society of Antiquaries in Scotland in 1894. Significantly, it was found to be inscribed with the effigy of St Clement's Church, Rodel.[8]

Today, the square tower of St Clement's remains a landmark of the Isles. Symbolic of the faith which inspired its creation, it stands above the rock bound harbour, defiant as was once the warrior chief of Harris who now lies resplendent in his tomb.

St Magnus Cathedral, Orkney
The Mariner's Church

The sky was very black. The wind was dropping but the storm continued to hold the night in its thrall. The cruel strength of the ocean surged against jagged rocks. The savage forces of nature were loosed in destructive rage.

The frail coracle of the pilgrims rounded a headland and in the same instant St Magnus Cathedral was outlined against the skyline, its lights glowing in the darkness, standing in glory revealed. Below lay the sheltered harbour of Kirkwall to which, like so many other voyagers over 800 years, they were guided in from the wastes of the sea by the landmark of the great church.

The cathedral dates from the 11th century when both Shetland and Orkney, together with Caithness on mainland Scotland, were under Norse rule. The Earls of Orkney, vassals of the King of Norway, acknowledged his superiority. Most powerful amongst them was Thorfinn the Mighty, son of Sigurd, whose wife was the daughter of Malcolm II of Scotland.

Following the death of Thorfinn, c.1068, his sons, Erlend and Paul, bore joint rule over Orkney. They seem to have defied authority for, in 1098, King Magnus arrived with a large fleet and promptly despatched them back to Norway.

He then forced Magnus, the young son of Erlend, to sail with him on his flagship on a voyage to the limits of his realm. He raided the Hebrides, then headed south for Anglesey to anchor in the Menai Strait. The Welsh sailed out to defy him and King Magnus ordered an attack. His men leapt to the battle stations, their axes sharpened to kill, but young Magnus Erlendson, saying he had no quarrel with any man, refused to fight. The

King raged in fury but Magnus sang hymns from his psalter as the battle raged around him and blood ran across the decks.

Later, under cover of darkness, Magnus escaped. He took refuge with his cousin, King Edgar of Scotland, until, following the death of his father, Earl Erlend, he returned to Orkney. Reaching home he found that his first cousin Hakon, son of his uncle Paul, had seized his father's share of land. Magnus, the man of peace, did not want to protest, but was eventually persuaded to claim his rights.

A year later, in 1104, Magnus married Ingarth, a Scottish noblewoman. The story goes that he plunged into a cold bath to cool his passion whenever he felt enamoured of her. The fact of there being no children lends some credence to this tale.

Inevitably, with two earls on Orkney, rivalry developed between their supporters. Wise men suggested a parley and the little island of Egilsay, which as Bishopric land was neutral territory, was chosen as a meeting place. The cousins agreed to sail there with only two ships each and escorts of a limited number of men.

Magnus reached Egilsay on 16 April 1117, shortly after Easter. Then seeing no less than eight ships approach the island he knew himself betrayed. He prayed quietly in the church as men swarmed ashore until, surrounded by his enemies, he begged that his life might be spared. 'God knows that I am looking more to your souls than to my life,' he told Hakon. 'Maim my body as thou likest, or pluck out my eyes and put me in a darksome dungeon.'

Hakon, shaken by his courage, was hesitant, but his followers clamoured that Magnus must die. However, when Ofeig, the standard bearer was chosen to be the executioner, he refused to do the awful deed so Hakon turned to Lifolf, his cook. The huge man wept but Magnus gave him his tunic and told him to 'Stand before me and hew on my head a great wound, for it is not seemly to behead chiefs like thieves. Take good heart, poor wretch, for I have prayed to God for thee.' The cook swung his great axe and Magnus died as it fell.

Magnus was buried at Egilsay, but his mother, Thora, commanded that his body be removed to Christ's Church at Birsay.[9] Later, as then was permitted, he was canonised by popular acclaim. Afterwards, a heavenly light was seen above his grave. Men in peril praying to him were saved and miraculous cures of illness were reported.

In 1314, a horseman in shining armour, thought to be the ghost of St Magnus, appeared in Aberdeen to announce the victory of Bannockburn. In 1513, on the day of King James IV's defeat at Flodden, his spirit manifested itself in the bay of Auchmeddan in Aberdeenshire (known as St Magnus Haven) and blessed the harbour so that the boats belonging to it should not be lost at sea.

There is also the famous story that, 16 years later, the apparition of St Magnus is claimed to have appeared to help the Orcadians repulse invaders from Caithness.

Back in 1129 the King of Norway granted the part of Orkney, which had belonged to the saint, to Kali Kolson, son of Magnus's sister Gunnhild and therefore legally his heir.

Kali, who had grown up in Norway, changed his name to 'Rognvald' before setting out to claim his inheritance in Orkney. The mission was ill-fated, as most of his ships were captured in Shetland and he returned to Norway in a state of deep depression.

His father, Kol, persuaded him to try again and this time he vowed that, should he win, he would build 'a church of stone in Kirkwall . . . more magnificent [than any] in the land and dedicated to his uncle St Magnus.' This expedition was successful and Rognvald, true to his promise, laid the foundation of St Magnus Cathedral, on 12 December (Santa Lucia's Day) 1137, just 20 years after his uncle was slain.[10]

The master masons came from Durham and similarities between the two cathedrals provide proof of their work. Red sandstone, to create the great pillars, was quarried from cliffs at Head of Holland, near Kirkwall, while the yellow sandstone which contrasts so beautifully where it is interlaid, probably came from the island of Eday. The work was supervised by Rognvald's father, Kol, who settled in Orkney with his son.

The western side of the (originally smaller) choir, the transepts and the nave, where the Norman round arches are so typical of the Romanesque style, comprise the oldest part of the church. The building proved more expensive than anticipated but Rognvald persuaded each farmer to contribute towards its completion. Thus, the cathedral was partly achieved by the people of Orkney themselves.

The Bishop of Orkney then was Bishop William, known for his great longevity as 'William the Old'. His predecessors had lived in Birsay but he is believed to have built the now ruined Bishop's Palace which stands close to the cathedral. During his time, in 1154, Orkney was placed under the Norwegian Bishop of Trondheim and remained so until 1472 when it became part of the Province of St Andrews.

Statues of Kol, the supervisor; Rognvald, the founder; and Bishop William the Old stand below the great east window of the choir.

Once the cathedral was consecrated, the bones of St Magnus were removed from Birsay and re-interred in a tomb before the altar at the east end of the choir. During the Reformation, however, monuments had to be removed and the sacred relics disappeared.

They lay forgotten until, in 1919, workmen doing repairs noticed that some of the stones in the column of the south arcade of the choir were loose. Pulling them out they found, to their astonishment, a cavity containing a casket. The box held most of the bones of a human skeleton, including, amazingly, a skull nearly cloven in two. St Magnus, rediscovered, was then replaced with reverence in the hole.

Likewise the remains of Earl Rognvald, also canonised after his death, were discovered in the corresponding pillar on the north side of the choir. Metal plaques now indicate the resting place of both saints.

The cathedral was enlarged towards the end of the 12th century with the addition of chapels at either end of the transepts. Afterwards, about 100 years later, the choir was extended to the east. The columns are finer and more ornamented than those of the original edifice – possibly thanks to French influence – but the red sandstone of the building glows as if with life blood as the mighty pillars soar upwards taking one's spirit to the heights.

Work was probably in progress during the winter of 1263 when King Hakon of Norway, his fleet scattered by gales after the battle of Largs, reached Orkney. He died in the Bishop's Palace.

Here also, according to tradition, the little Maid of Norway, granddaughter of Alexander III, died from the effects of measles (and a dreadful sea-crossing), in the arms of the Bishop of Bergen in 1290.[11]

During the 13th century, plans were made to extend the cathedral to the west. The three

great doorways, built at this time, are thought
to have stood apart like sentinels for about
200 years until eventually, at the end of the
15th century, they were joined to the
extension of the nave.

In 1467 both Orkney and Shetland were
ceded to Scotland as part of the dowry of the
Princess Margaret, daughter of Christian I of
Norway, who married James III of Scotland.
On 20 February 1472, parliament annexed the
earldom of Orkney and Shetland to the
crown, the Earl of Orkney being compensated
for his loss. The King bequeathed St Magnus
Cathedral to the people of Kirkwall in 1486.
Now the property of the Orkney Islands
Council, it remains a parish church.

The tower, dating from the 14th century,
holds the three great bells, gifted by Bishop
Robert Maxwell in the reign of James V. Still
rung with the old Norse method of clocking,
they peal out over Kirkwall as they have done
for over 450 years. Disaster struck in 1671,
however, when the tower was struck by
lightning and the bells crashed to the ground.
The largest, badly cracked, had to be recast in
Amsterdam. Eight years passed before the
spire was replaced with the help of
neighbouring parishes. A new spire cast in
copper was erected in the 1920s when stained
glass was put into most of the windows.[12]

The Earl's Palace, which also stands close
to the cathedral, retains the beauty of its
structure, despite its largely ruined state. Built
c.1607 by Earl Patrick Stewart, son of an

illegitimate son of James V, after he had obtained the Bishopric, it was seized by Stewart's enemy Bishop Law. Stewart was imprisoned in Dumbarton Castle for his savagery towards the people of Orkney in 1614. His son, Robert, then arrived in the islands, captured the cathedral and installed men within the tower.

The Earl of Caithness, on the King's authority, tried to have the tower pulled down but was prevented by Bishop Law. Some of the rebels may have been consigned to Marwick's Hole, the dungeon between the south wall of the choir and the south transept chapel. The hangman's double ladder still lies significantly in the nave.

Maintenance of the cathedral has continued over the years. The greatest single benefactor was George Thoms, Sheriff of Caithness, Orkney and Shetland from 1890–98, who bequeathed the then enormous sum of £60,000. An investment of £9,000 provided a fabric fund but in 1958 it became necessary to form the Society of the Friends of St Magnus to raise money for repairs.

In 1965 St Rognvald's Chapel was designated in the east end of the choir. Decorated panels of the 16th and 17th centuries contrast with the pulpit, communion table and lectern which, designed by Stanley Cursiter, an Orcadian and the Queen's Painter and Limner in Scotland, were carved by Reynold Eunson, a local man.

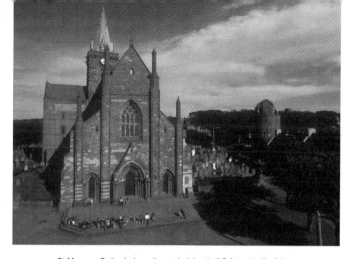

St Magnus Cathedral, on the main island of Orkney, built of the beautiful local red sandstone by masons from Durham, c.1137, and dedicated to St Magnus, whose cloven skull lies buried in one of the south arcades of the choir

In 1971 came a bombshell as an architect, asked to survey the fabric of the cathedral, reported that the west end of the nave was in great danger of collapse.

A 'Save St Magnus' Appeal Committee was organised by the Town Council of Kirkwall. The Lord Lieutenant of Orkney, Colonel Sir Robert Macrae was Chairman, and Her Majesty Queen Elizabeth, the Queen Mother, became Patron. An appeal for £300,000, launched by Lord Birsay, met with a generous response and a Service of Thanksgiving was held in 1974 to celebrate the rescue of the cathedral.

On 9 August 1987 the glorious new west window, commissioned by the Friends of the Cathedral to mark the 850th anniversary of its foundation, was unveiled by Her Majesty the Queen. The artist, Crear McCartney, has depicted Orkney motifs of the past and the present, with the battle-axe significant of the martyrdom of Magnus surmounting the Dove of Peace. To mark the ocassion, the Hordaland Council of Norway presented the people of Orkney with a white tapestry. The design of a sail is symbolic of the long friendship between Norway and Orkney.

Burials continued to take place within the cathedral until the middle of the last century. The oldest grave slab of the 13th century, bearing a cross and a sword, stands in the choir. Most are 17th century as is the macabre wooden memorial called the 'Mort Brod' (Death Board) showing a shrouded skeleton hanging in the nave. Most poignant of all memorials is the plaque in honour of the men of HMS *Royal Oak*, sunk by a submarine in Scapa Flow at the onset of the Second World War in 1939 – victims, as was St Magnus, of man's inhumanity to man.

The Festival of St Magnus, held within the cathedral each June, springs from the inspiration of the composer Sir Peter Maxwell Davies and the Orcadian poet George Mackay Brown. Glorious music soars to the roof with the power of a surging sea.

The cathedral remains the hub of the community as it has been throughout the years. Created by Earl Rognvald, whose faith and perseverance turned failure into success, St Magnus Cathedral stands defiant of destruction by time and the fury of the elements, in glorious testimony of the power of the Christian faith.

BIBLIOGRAPHY

A.P.S. *Acts of Parliament*, V

Acta Sanctorum, 1865 ed

Adomnan, St, *Life of St Columba* (edited by Anderson, A.O. & M.O. Thomas), Nelson & Sons Ltd, Edinburgh, 1961

Balfour-Melville, E.W.M., *James I King of Scots*, Methuen & Co. Ltd, London, 1936

Breviarum Aberdonense (Aberdeen Breviary), Edinburgh 1510, translated A.O. Anderson, reprinted by Spalding & Maitland Clubs, 1854

Brooke, D., *The Search for St Ninian*, Friends of the Whithorn Trust, Mansfield, 1990

Brooke, D., *Wild Men and Holy Places*, Canongate, 1994

Catholic Encyclopedia

Celtic Review, vol. iii

Chadwick, N.K., *The Age of the Saints in the Early Celtic Church*, Oxford University Press, London, 1961

Chambers, W.R., *The Domestic Annals of Scotland from the Reformation to the Revolution*, 3 vols, Edinburgh, 1874

Chronicle of the Picts and Scots

Collins Encyclopedia of Scotland (ed. J. & J. Keay), Harper Collins, London, 1994

Croal's Sketches of East Lothian

Cruden, Stewart, *Scottish Medieval Churches*, John Donald Ltd, Edinburgh, 1986

Duke of Argyll in Scott. Eccles, Soc. Trans, V (1915)

Dunfermline, the Abbey and Palace of, Historic Scotland

Easson, D.E., *Medieval Religious Houses in Scotland,* Longmans, Green & Co., 1957

Edmonstone, Sir A., *Family of Edmonstone of Duntreath*, 1875

Fawcett, Richard, *Elgin Cathedral*, Historic Scotland, Edinburgh

Felize of Oengus

Forster, F.A., *Studies in Church Dedications*

Gibbon and Ross, *Ecclesiastical Architecture of Scotland*

Gilles, Revd.,W.S., *In Famed Breadalbane,* Clunie Press, Perthshire, 1938

Gregory, D., *History of the Western Highlands and Isles of Scotland from 1493 to 1625*, William Tait, Edinburgh

Henry, F., *Irish Art in the Romanesque Period*

Holmes, Dom Augustine, *Pluscarden Abbey*, Historic Scotland, 2004

Holyrood Ordinale c.1450

Johnston, J.A., *Tongue and Farr,* Sutherland, 1997

Joynso, P., *Local Past*, 1996

Knight, G.A. Frank, *Archaelogical Light on the Early Christianizing of Scotland*, 2 vols, James Clarke Ltd, London, 1933

Mackie, J.D.E., *A History of Scotland*, Penguin, 1964

MacKinlay, J.M., *Ancient Church Dedications in Scotland*, David Douglas, Edinburgh

MacQuarrie, A., *The Saints of Scotland*, John Donald Publishers Ltd, Edinburgh, 1997

MacRae, K., (Coinneach Mor) *Northern Narrative*, 1955

McCarg, R., *Govan Parish Church*

Mitchison, R.A., *History of Scotland*, Methuen & Co., London, 1970

Moffat, A., *Before Scotland*, Thames & Hudson, 2005

Mooney, Revd. H., *St Magnus Cathedral, Orkney*

Murray, W.H., *The Islands of Western Scotland*, Eyre Methuen, London, 1973

New Statistical Account of Scotland, Aberdeen, William Blackwood & Sons, Edinburgh & London

Ibid *Argyle*

Nicholson, R., *Scotland the Late Middle Ages*, Mercat Press, Edinburgh

O'Reilly, K.J., *What to see in Strathnaver*, local guide book

Orkneyinga Saga

Presbytery Book of Strathbogie, extracts from

Royal Commission of the Ancient & Historical Monuments of Scotland (R.C.A.H.M.S.), vols. 1–5 & 7, H.M.S.O. Press, Edinburgh

R.M.S., *Registrum Magni Sigilli Regnum Scotorium, 1882-1914*

Skene, W.F., *Celtic Scotland – A History of Ancient Alban*, vol. ii, David Douglas, Edinburgh, 1887

Slade, H.G., *The Collegiate Kirk of St Duthac of Tain and the Abbey of Fern*, Tain & District Museum Trust, 2000

Steer, K.A.S. & J.W.M. Bannerman, *Late Medieval Monumental Sculpture in the West Highlands*, R.C.A.H.M.S., Edinburgh, 1997

Stokes, W. (ed), *Martyrology of Gorman*, 1895

Sugden, K., *Walking the Pilgrim Ways*, David & Charles, 1991

Temple, Revd Dr, *The Thaneage of Fermartyn*

Thomas, C., *Whithorn's Christian Beginnings*, First Whithorn Lecture, 1992

Traquair, P., *Freedom's Sword*, Harper Collins, 1998

Undiscovered Scotland: The ultimate online guide to Whithorn

Wardlaw, *Chronicle of the Frasers (Wardlaw Manuscript)*, 1905

Watson, W.J., *Place Names of Ross & Cromarty*

Yeoman, P., *Pilgrimage in Medieval Scotland*, Batsford/Historic Scotland, 1999

NOTES

Introduction
1 Skene, W.F., *Celtic Scotland*, vol. ii, pp.6–7
2 R.C.A.H.M.S., *Argyll*, vol. i, *Kintyre*, pp.145–47
3 Ibid, vol. iv, *Iona*, pp.204–8
4 Ibid, vol. v, pp.209–12
5 R.C.A.H.M.S., *Argyll*, vol. iii, p.147

All Roads Lead to Rome
1 MacKinlay, J.M., *Ancient Church Dedications (scriptual) in Scotland*, pp.237–9
2 Thomas, Charles, *Whithorn's Christian Beginnings*, p.10
3 Brooke, D., *The Search for St Ninian*, p.9
4 Brooke, D., *Wild Men and Holy Places*, pp.181–183
5 Now in the Royal National Museum in Edinburgh

Pilgrims of the River Clyde
1 Knight, G.A.F., *Archaelogical Light . . .*, vol. i, pp.152–4
2 Mackinlay, J.M., *Ancient Church Dedications (non scriptual) in Scotland*, pp.101–2
3 MacQuarrie, A., *The Saints of Scotland*, p.4
4 Knight, G.A.F., *Archaelogical Light . . .*, vol. i, p.324-35
5 Simpson, W.D., *The Historical St Columba*, p.44
6 Yeoman, P., *Pilgrimage in Medieval Scotland*, pp.22–3
7 *Breviarum Aberdonense* (Aberdeen Breviary)
8 Yeoman, P., *Pilgrimage in Medieval Scotland*, pp.28–9
9 Knight, G.A.F., *Archaelogical Light . . .*, pp.62–3
10 Yeoman, P., *Pilgrimage in Medieval Scotland*, p.28
11 Grant, I.F., *The Lordship of the Isles*, p.362
12 *Breviarum Aberdonense*
13 See *Govan Parish Church* by Rosemary McCarg. Also *Govan Old Parish Church 2001* Information Leaflet
14 Knight, G.A.F., *Archaelogical Light . . .*, p.67
15 Yeoman, P., *Pilgrimage in Medieval Scotland*, p.30
16 Mackinlay, J.M., *Ancient Church Dedications (non scriptual)*, p.267
17 Yeoman, P., *Pilgrimage in Medieval Scotland*, p.32
18 Knight, G.A.F., *Archaelogical Light . . .*, vol. ii, p.104
19 Duke of Argyll in Scott Eccles. Soc. Trans. V. (1915), p.65
20 *Breviarum Aberdonense*, Pars hyem. Fol.lx. b. lxi
21 Dalyell, *The Darker Superstitions of Scotland* (1834), p.151

Saints of the Highlands & Islands
1 *Adomnan's Life of Columba*, ed. A. Anderson, p.195
2 R.C.A.H.M.S., *Argyll*, vol. vii, pp.200–1
3 *Adomnan's Life of Columba*, p.107, 154, 197, 385-9, 401, 409
4 R.C.A.H.M.S., *Argyll*, vol. iii, pp.153–8
5 Knight, G.A.F., *Archaelogical Light . . .*, vol. ii, p.31

6 *Felire of Oengus*, p.117
7 Knight, G.A.F., *Archaelogical Light . . .*, vol. ii, p.96
8 Watson, W.J., *Place-Names of Ross and Cromarty*, p.193
9 Knight, G.A.F., *Archaelogical Light . . .*, vol. ii, p.99
10 R.C.A.H.M.S., *Argyll*, vol. ii, 'Lorn', pp.156–71
11 Ibid, p.161
12 Simpson, W.D., *The Historical Saint Columba*, p.1
13 R.C.A.H.M.S., vol. v, p.184; vol. vii, p.120, 159, 161
14 Ibid, vol. ii, pp. 144–5
15 Knight, G.A.F., *Archaelogical Light . . .*, vol. ii, p.71-3
16 *Family of Edmonstone of Dunreath*, pub. privately, 1861
17 Easson, D.E., *Medieval Religious Houses*, p.158, 168
18 Dewar = the Gaelic name for custodian
19 Easson, D.E., *Medieval Religious Houses*, p.83
20 Ibid, p.125
21 R.C.A.H.M.S., *Argyll*, vol. ii, pp. 121, 134–5. Sited on the loch side of the A819, the building is now a private house
22 Duke of Argyll in Scott Eccles. Soc. Trans. V. (1915), p.55
23 Knight, G.A.F., *Archaelogical Light . . .*, vol. ii, p.354
24 Slade, G.H., *The Collegiate Kirk of St Duthac of Tain*, p.8
25 MacQuarrie, A., *The Saints of Scotland*, p.147

Shrines of the Forth Valley & Tay
1 Skene, W.F., *Celtic Scotland*, vol. ii, pp.256–8
2 Knight, G.A.F., *Archaelogical Light . . .*, vol. i, p.294
3 Easson, D.E., *Medieval Religious Houses*, p.78 & 153
4 Knight, G.A.F., *Archaelogical Light . . .*, vol. ii, p.268–9
5 Easson, D.E., *Medieval Religious Houses*, p.78
6 Skene, W.F., *Celtic Scotland*, vol. ii, p.223
7 Balfour-Melville, E.W.M., *James I, King of Scots*, p.30
8 Mackinlay, J.M., *Ancient Church Dedications*, p.19
9 Yeoman, P., *Pilgrimage in Medieval Scotland*, p.63
10 Easson, D.E., *Medieval Religious Houses*, p.53-4
11 *Chronicle of the Picts and Scots*, p.423. Also Skene, *Celtic Scotland*, vol. ii
12 Gibbon & Ross, *Ecclesiastical Architecture of Scotland*, vol. iii, p.272
13 Mackinlay, J.M., *Ancient Church Dedications . . .*, p.95
14 *Croal's Sketches of East Lothian*, p.178
15 Balfour-Melville, E.W.M., *James I King of Scots*, p.236
16 Easson, D.E., *Medieval Religious Houses*, p.145
17 *Catholic Encyclopedia*
18 Yeoman, P., *Pilgrimage in Medieval Scotland*, pp.111-12

Healing Wells
1 MacRae, K., (Coinneach Mor) *Northern Narrative*
2 Knight, G.A.F., *Archaelogical Light . . .*, vol. ii, p.235
3 Yeoman, P., *Pilgrimage in Medieval Scotland*, p.99–100
4 Knight, G.A.F., *Archaelogical Light . . .*, vol. ii, p.236
5 Holyrood ordinale. Also *Collins Encyclopedia of Scotland*
6 *Extracts from the Presbytery Book of Strathbogie*

The Great Abbeys & Cathedrals

1 Yeoman, P., *Pilgrimage in Medieval Scotland*, p.45
2 *Catholic Encyclopedia*
3 R.M.S., ii, nos. 331, 430
4 R.M.S., nos. 379, 380
5 Yeoman, P., *Pilgrimage in Medieval Scotland*, p.46
6 *Collins Encyclopedia of Scotland*, p.391
7 *Catholic Encyclopedia*
8 Queen Margaret's chaplain, Archdeacon and then Prior of Durham, later became Bishop of St Andrews
9 Mackinlay, J.M., *Ancient Church Dedications in Scotland (non scriptual)*, pp.339–40
10 *The Abbey and Palace of Dunfermline*, p.15
11 Mackinlay, J.M., *Ancient Church Dedications in Scotland (non scriptual)*, pp.6–8
12 Knight, G.A.F., *Archaeological Light . . .*, vol. ii, p.269-70
13 Skene, W.F., *Celtic Scotland*, vol. ii, p.274
14 Cruden, S., *Scottish Medieval Churches*, p.15-18
15 See Yeoman, P., *Pilgrimage in Medieval Scotland* (pp.57–62) for more details on the ferry crossing
16 Mackinlay, J.M., *Ancient Church Dedications*, pp.337–8
17 Cruden, S., *Scottish Medieval Churches*, p.150-2
18 Mackinlay, J.M., *Ancient Church Dedications in Scotland (non scriptual)*, p.113
19 Knight, G.A.F., *Archaeological Light . . .*, vol. ii, pp.230–31
20 Skene, W.F., *Celtic Scotland*, vol. ii, p.230
21 Easson, D.E., *Medieval Religious Houses*, p.83
22 APS, IV. 328. Also, RMS, IV. No. 2138
23 Knight, G.A.F., *Archaeological Light . . .*, vol. ii, pp.232–4
24 Ibid., vol. ii, pp.287-30
25 R.C.A.H.M.S., *Argyll*, vol. ii, pp.160
26 *Undiscovered Scotland*, the online guide
27 *Collins Encyclopedia of Scotland*, pp.351–2
28 Elgin Cathedral, Collection of Papers, ed. R. Fawcett
29 Holmes, Don Augustine, *Guidebook of Pluscarden*, 2004
30 Wardlaw M.S.S., *Chronicle of the Frasers* (1905), p.468
31 Mackinlay, J.M., *Ancient Church Dedications*, p.325

Sacred Treasures of the Isles

1 Henry, F., *Irish Art . . .*, pp.7–8, 192, 205–8
2 R.C.A.H.M.S., vol. iv, p.143
3 Ibid, p.107
4 R.C.A.H.M.S., vol. v, p.252
5 *Celtic Review*, vol. iii, p 251
6 See Steer & Bannerman, *Late Medieval Monumental Sculpture in the West Highlands*, pp.78–81 & pp.180–82
7 Murray, W.H., *The Islands of Western Scotland*, p.274
8 Mackinlay, J.M., *Ancient Church Dedications*, p.290
9 Cruden, S., *Scottish Medieval Churches*, p.115
10 Mooney, The Rev. H., *St Magnus Cathedral, Orkney*
11 Mackie, J.D., *A History of Scotland*, p.105
12 Mooney, The Rev. H., *St Magnus Cathedral, Orkney*

INDEX